THE LIFE OF
JESUS
CHRIST

The Gospel of Mark

J. WESLEY EBY, EDITOR

f

THE FOUNDRY
PUBLISHING®

ISBN 978-0-8341-3989-3

Printed in the United States of America

Cover Design: Paul Franitza

10 9 8 7 6 5 4 3

CONTENTS

Teaching Resources

PRONUNCIATION GUIDE

Symbol	Key Words	Usual Letters	Symbol	Key Words	Usual Letters
ay	age, day	a, ai, ay	b	boat, cab	b, bb
a	ask, cat	a	ch	church, match	ch, tch
ah	father, ox	a, o	d	day, dad	d, dd
aw	auto, saw	a, au, aw	f	foot, wife	f, ff, ph,
ee	each, see	e, ee, ea, ey,	gh		
y			g	gate, big	g, gg
e	egg, bed	e	h	hand, behind	h, wh
air	pair, bear	air, are, ear	j	joy, page	j, g, dg
er	her, bird	er, ir, ur	k	king, music	k, c, ck, ch
ie	ice, pie	i, ie, y	ks	box, sacks	x, cks
i	inch, sit	i	kw	queen, equal	qu
oh	oat, no	o, oa, oe, ow	l	life, hill	l, ll
ew	new, moon	u, ew, oo, ue	m	man, ham	m, mm
oo	good, bush	oo, u	n	new, son	n, nn, kn
ou	out, cow	ou, ow	ng	drink, sing	n, ng
oy	oil, boy	oi, oy	p	pig, cap	p, pp
yew	use, human	u	r	race, year	r, rr, wr
u*	up, just	u	s	sun, face	s, c, ss, sc
uh*	mother, ago	any vowel	sh	sheep, fish	sh, ti
			t	teach, mat	t, tt
			th	thin, bath	th
			<u>th</u>	this, bathe	th
			v	vine, love	v
			w	win, away	w
			y	you, beyond	y
			z	zeal, bees	z, zz, s
			zh	measure	s, z

*This is the same as the schwa sound found
in many dictionaries.

INTRODUCTION

This book is for people who are learning English. This book is also for people learning to read. The words and sentences are short. The lessons are not long. You should be able to understand the lessons.

The writers want you to know about God. They want you to know about Jesus Christ. And they want you to understand what you are learning. This is why the book was written.

In this book, you will learn about Jesus Christ. You will learn that He is the Son of God. You will learn some important things about His life. You will learn some things that He taught. You will learn why He came to earth.

In this book, you can also learn how to become a Christian. Are you a Christian already? If you are a Christian, that is great. If you are not a Christian, you can be. Turn to lesson 29 on page 63. This lesson can help you receive Jesus as your Savior.

Your pastor or teacher will help you learn. They want you to know about God. They want you to know Jesus Christ. They want you to understand the Bible. They want you to be a Christian. And they want you to grow as a Christian.

Would you ask your pastor or teacher for help? Ask them about the things you do not know. Ask them about the things you do not understand. Ask them to pray with you about becoming a Christian. They will be glad to help you.

You can pray to God. He will help you understand. He will help you learn. He will help you believe in Jesus, His Son. God will help you become a Christian. He will help you grow as a Christian.

God loves you very much. He wants to be your God. He wants you to believe in His Son, Jesus Christ. God wants you to be a Christian. He wants you to be His child.

1 MARK TELLS ABOUT JESUS CHRIST

Memory Verse: "... believe the **good news!**" (Mark 1:15)
Scripture: Mark 1:1

The **Holy Bible** tells us about God. The **Holy Bible** also tells us about Jesus Christ. Four of the books are about the life of Jesus. We call these books the **Gospels**. These books tell us the **good news** about Jesus.

A man named Mark wrote one of these books. The name of the book is *Mark*. The other books are *Matthew* (MATH-yew), *Luke*, and *John*. These books are the **Gospels**.

Mark lived while Jesus lived. Mark was a friend of Peter (PEE-ter). Peter worked with Jesus Christ. Peter saw what Jesus did. He heard what Jesus said. Mark wrote the things that Peter told him about Jesus.

Other **Gospels** tell about the birth of Jesus. Jesus was born in a town called Bethlehem (BETH-luh-hem). He lived in a town called Nazareth (NAZ-uh-ruhth). He obeyed His parents, Mary and Joseph. He worked with His father. He studied the **Scripture**.

Mark began the story of Jesus when Jesus was 30 years old. Mark told what Jesus did. Jesus was doing the **work of God** on earth. Jesus helped other people. He helped people with all types of problems. He helped sick people. Jesus also used His power to stop storms.

Jesus taught us how to live. And He showed us how to live. Jesus showed us how to love other people. He showed us how to love **ourselves**.

Jesus can **forgive** our **sins**. Jesus showed us how to **forgive** other people. He showed us how to **forgive ourselves**.

The *Gospel of Mark* tells the **good news** about Jesus. Jesus Christ is the Son of God. Jesus came to **save** us from our **sins**. Jesus came to show us the love of God. He helps us to love God more than anything else.

Mark wanted us to know Jesus. Mark wrote his book to help us. We can learn about Jesus Christ as we study *Mark*. Jesus wants to **save** us from our **sins**. We can learn this **good news.**

QUESTIONS: *Fill in the blanks.*

1. Four books in the **Holy Bible** are about the life of

   _____.

2. These books tell us the _____

   _____ about Jesus. He came to **save** us from

   our_____.

3. A man named _____ wrote one of the **Gospels**.

4. Mark wrote the things Peter said about_____.

5. Jesus was born in a town called_____.

6. Jesus studied the _____.

Answer with YES or NO. Circle the right answer.

7. Did Jesus do the **work of God** on earth?   YES or NO

8. Does Mark tell the bad news about Jesus Christ?   YES or NO

9. Is Jesus the Son of God?   YES or NO

10. Can Jesus **forgive** our **sins**?   YES or NO

WORD LIST

1. **forgive** *(verb):* make free from the shame for **sins**; choose to forget the wrong things that people do.

2. **good news** *(noun phrase):* the story that Jesus Christ can **save** people from their **sins**.

3. **Gospel, Gospels** *(proper noun):* the first four books of the New Testament in the Bible. (The **Gospels** tell the **good news** about Jesus Christ. **Gospel** means "good news.")

4. **Holy Bible** *(proper noun):* the 66 books that God gave us to learn about Him; the written Word of God; the **Scripture**.

5. **ourselves** *(pronoun):* us; the same persons as you and me.

6. **save** *(verb):* make free from **sin**; not punish people for their **sins**.

7. **Scripture** *(proper noun):* the **Holy Bible**; the written Word of God; any part of the Bible.

8. **sin, sins** *(noun):* the acts and thoughts of people against God and His laws; the things people do when they do not obey God.

9. **work of God** *(noun phrase):* anything that God tells people to do; what God does to help people know and love Him.

2 JESUS CHRIST IS THE SON OF GOD

Memory Verse: "You are my Son, whom I love . . . " (Mark 1:11)
Scripture: Mark 1:11
Background Scripture: Mark 1:4-10

God is our Father. He made us. He loves us very much. God wants to help His people. God sent Jesus to earth to help us.

The Holy Bible tells us about the birth of Jesus. You can read about His birth in the Gospel of Luke. (Luke 2:1-20)

Jesus had a human mother. Her name was Mary. Jesus did not have a human father. God is the Father of Jesus. The birth of Jesus was a **miracle**. He was both the Son of God and **Son of Man**.

Mark had a **message** for all people. The **message** was that Jesus is the Son of God. Many people knew Jesus. But they did not think that Jesus was the Son of God. They did not know about His **miracle** birth. Many people thought Jesus was just a good man.

Mark said that God sent a special **preacher**. That special **preacher** was a man named John. He also had a **message**. John said that people must **repent** of their sins. Then, John **baptized** the people who **repented**. This preacher was called John the Baptist.

John preached that Jesus Christ would come soon. John preached that Jesus Christ had more power than John had. Jesus had power to do **miracles**. He was more important than John was. John **baptized** people with water. But Jesus would **baptize** with the **Holy Spirit**.

The **message** and work of John was very important. He said some important things. He preached that people must **repent** of their sins. He preached that Jesus Christ would come.

One day, Jesus went to see John. John **baptized** Jesus in the Jordan (JOHR-dun) River. Then, the **Holy Spirit** came down on Jesus from **heaven**. The **Holy Spirit** looked like a **dove**.

Next, a voice came from **heaven** with a **message**. The voice said, "You are My Son, whom I love . . ." (verse 11) The voice was the voice of God. God called Jesus "My Son." God was telling everyone that Jesus was His Son.

Jesus Christ is the Son of God. And Jesus is the **Son of Man**. Only Jesus is God and man together. This is an important **message**. Do you believe it?

QUESTIONS: *Fill in the blanks.*

1. God is our _____. He _____ us very much.
2. _____ was the mother of Jesus. _____ is the Father of Jesus.
3. Jesus is the _____ of _____.
4. John said that people must _____ of their sins.
5. John said that Jesus Christ would _____ soon.
6. _____ **baptized** Jesus in the Jordan River.
7. The _____ _____ came down on Jesus. He looked like a bird that we call a **dove**.
8. God called Jesus "_____ _____."
9. **Heaven** is the home of _____. **Heaven** is also the home for _____ after death.
10. Only _____ is God and man together. Only Jesus is both the Son of God and the _____ _____ _____.

WORD LIST

1. **background Scripture** *(noun phrase):* some Scripture from the Bible; other Scripture to help us better understand the lesson.
2. **baptize, baptized** *(verb):* put under water and lifted out of water.
3. **dove** *(noun):* a type of small bird that is white or gray.
4. **heaven** *(noun):* the home of God. (**Heaven** is also where Christians live after death.)
5. **Holy Spirit** *(proper noun):* the Spirit of God.
6. **message** *(noun):* a written or spoken way to share some news.
7. **miracle, miracles** *(noun):* something that happens only with the help of God; something that people cannot do without the power of God.
8. **preacher** *(noun):* a person who tells other people about God; a person who tells the good news of Jesus. (A **preacher** often speaks or preaches in a church.)
9. **repent, repented** *(verb):* stop doing sins; turn from a life of sin and turn to God.
10. **Son of Man** *(proper noun phrase):* Jesus Christ, who was born of a human mother.

3 SATAN TEMPTED JESUS

Memory Verse: ". . . He [Jesus] is able to help those who are being
   tempted." (Hebrews 2:18)
Scripture: Mark 1:12-13
Background Scripture: Matthew 4:1-11

The Spirit of God sent Jesus Christ into the desert. Jesus was in
the desert 40 days. He did not eat anything. He was very hungry.

Satan came to Jesus and **tempted** Him. **Satan** knew that Jesus
was the Son of God. **Satan** told Jesus to make bread from stones.
Then, Jesus would have food to eat. But He did not obey **Satan.**
Instead, Jesus said Scripture to **Satan.**

Satan tempted Jesus Christ again. **Satan** took Jesus to the top
of a tall building. **Satan** told Jesus to jump off. **Satan** said that God
would not let Jesus be hurt. But Jesus did not obey **Satan.** Again,
Jesus said Scripture to **Satan.**

Satan tempted Jesus one more time. **Satan tempted** Jesus to
worship Satan. But, Jesus knew that God wants us to **worship** only
God. Jesus said "no" to the **temptation.** Again, Jesus said Scripture
to **Satan.**

Jesus Christ chose not to sin. He knew God could help Him.
Jesus obeyed God. Jesus said "no" to all the **temptations.** Then,
Satan went away.

Sometimes, people **turn away from God.** It is a sin to **turn away
from God. Satan tempts** us to **turn away from God.** Sometimes,
Satan tempts us with bad things. Sometimes, **Satan tempts** us with
things that seem good.

One day, we may need some money. A friend has money, and
we want his or her money. **Satan** may **tempt** us to steal the money.
But we should not steal the money. It is a sin to steal.

Satan tempts all people. Everyone has **temptations.** But a
temptation is not a sin. Yet, it is a sin to say "yes" to a **temptation.**
We should say "no" to it. We should never say "yes" to
temptations.

Jesus showed us how to say "no" to **temptations.** He showed us
how to obey God. We can say Scripture. We can pray. We should
not **worship Satan.** We should **worship** only God. Jesus will help us
when **Satan tempts** us.

QUESTIONS: *Fill in the blanks.*

1. Jesus Christ was in the _____ for 40 days.

2. _____ **tempted** Jesus three times.

3. Jesus Christ chose not to _____.

4. Jesus Christ said "no" to the _____ .

5. We should say "_____" to **temptation.**

Answer with YES or NO. Circle the right answer.

6. Could Jesus have made bread from stones?   YES or NO

7. Did **Satan tempt** Jesus only one time?   YES or NO

8. Does **Satan tempt** all people?   YES or NO

9. Is it a sin when **Satan tempts** us?   YES or NO

10. Will Jesus help us when **Satan tempts** us?   YES or NO

WORD LIST

1. **Satan** *(proper noun):* the very bad spirit who fights against God; the bad spirit with the most power.

2. **tempt, tempts, tempted** *(verb):* try to get a person to sin or do wrong.

3. **temptation, temptations** *(noun):* the act of **Satan** to **tempt** people; **Satan** trying to get a person to sin.

4. **turn away from God** *(verb phrase):* do not obey God; do not **worship** God any longer; sin against God.

5. **worship** *(verb):* obey and serve; give thanks to; give honor to.

4   PEOPLE FOLLOWED JESUS

Memory Verse: " 'Come, follow Me,' Jesus said . . ." (Mark 1:17)
Scripture: Mark 1:14-20

A bad king put John the Baptist in a jail. John had to stop preaching. Then, Jesus went to **Galilee** (GAL-uh-lee). Jesus began to preach the good news from God.

One day, Jesus walked near a large lake. He saw two brothers fishing. Their names were Peter and Andrew. They were **fishermen**. They threw their nets into the lake to catch fish.

Jesus said, "Come, follow Me." Peter and Andrew left their jobs as **fishermen**. They left Lake **Galilee**. They followed Jesus **quickly**.

Jesus walked near Lake **Galilee** again. He saw two more brothers. Their names were James and John. Their father was Zebedee (ZEB-uh-dee).

James and John were in their boat. Their father was with them. Other men worked for Zebedee. They were **fishermen**. They worked on their fish nets.

Jesus said to James and John, "Come, follow Me." James and John left their jobs. They left Lake **Galilee**. They followed Jesus **quickly**.

Today, we must follow Jesus too. We follow Jesus when we obey God. We follow Jesus when we do what God says.

How does God speak to us today? He speaks to us as we read the Holy Bible. The Bible is the truth of God for us.

God speaks to us when we pray. He will talk to us as we talk to Him. We must listen for His voice. We will hear His voice in our spirits.

God speaks to us as we listen to **sermons**. Our **pastors** study the Scripture. God helps our **pastors**. Our **pastors** preach **sermons** that we need to hear.

Peter, Andrew, James, and John heard Jesus call to them. They listened. And they followed Jesus **quickly**.

Is God speaking to you? Are you following Jesus?

QUESTIONS: *Give the answers.*

1. Where did Jesus begin to preach? _____
2. What did Jesus say to the **fishermen**? "Come, _____
   _____."
3. Who were the first men to follow Jesus? _____ and
   _____.
4. Who were two other brothers who followed Jesus?
   _____ and _____.
5. Who was the father of James and John? _____ .

Fill in the blanks.

6. Today, we must _____ Jesus too.
7. We follow Jesus when we _____ God.
8. God speaks to us when we read the _____.
9. The Holy Bible is the Word of _____.
10. God speaks to us as we listen to _____ .

WORD LIST

1. **fishermen** *(noun):* people who catch fish for a job.
2. **Galilee** *(proper noun):* a part of the country where Jesus lived; also, the name of a large lake in this country.
3. **pastors** *(noun):* people who preach about God. (**Pastors** often preach **sermons** in churches. **Pastors** are also preachers.)
4. **quickly** *(adverb):* fast; right away.
5. **sermons** *(noun):* messages; what **preachers** or **pastors** say when they tell us about God. (**Pastors** often preach **sermons** in church services.)

5   JESUS CAN FORGIVE SINS

Memory Verse: "Your sins are **forgiven**." (Mark 2:5)
Scripture: Mark 2:1-12

Jesus went to the city of Capernaum (kuh-PER-nee-um). The people knew that Jesus was there. Many people went to the house where He stayed. They wanted to hear Him preach.

More and more people came to hear Jesus. The house was full. No more people could get inside the house.

Four men carried a **paralyzed** man to the house. They had **faith** that Jesus could help the **paralyzed** man. The men could not get inside the house. So, they went up on the roof. They made a hole in the roof. They put the man down through the hole.

Jesus saw what the men did. Jesus knew they had **faith** in Him. He spoke to the man on the mat. Jesus said, "Your sins are **forgiven**. I forgive you of all your sins."

Some teachers of the law were in the house. They heard what Jesus said. The teachers thought, "Why did Jesus say that? Only God can forgive sins." They did not believe that Jesus could forgive sins.

Jesus said to them, "I can say, 'I forgive your sins.' Or I can say, 'Stand up. Take your mat. Walk!' Which is better? I will show you that I can forgive sins."

Jesus said to the **paralyzed** man, "Stand up. Take your mat and go home." The **paralyzed** man stood. He took his mat and walked home. Everyone watched him. Jesus had **healed** the man.

The people were surprised. Jesus **healed** the **paralyzed** man. They **praised** God. They said, "We have never seen anything like this!"

All people are born with sin. We need Jesus Christ to forgive our sins. Sin makes us think wrong thoughts. Sin makes us do wrong things.

Jesus will forgive our sins. He will help us think right. He will help us live right. We should **praise** God that He forgives us.

Jesus, the Son of God, can forgive our sins. And He can **heal** our bodies. But it is more important that Jesus forgives our sins.

Do you have **faith** that Jesus can forgive your sins? Do you have **faith** that He can **heal** your body?

QUESTIONS: *Give the answers.*

1. What city did Jesus go to? _____ .
2. Who went to hear Jesus? _____ .
3. How did four men help the **paralyzed** man get to Jesus? They put the man down through the _____.
4. What did Jesus know about the four men? They had great _____ in Him.
5. What did Jesus say to the **paralyzed** man? "I _____ your _____."
6. What else did Jesus do for the **paralyzed** man? Jesus _____ the man.

Answer with YES or NO. Circle the right answer.

7. Are all people born with sin?   YES or NO
8. Does sin make us do good things?   YES or NO
9. Will Jesus forgive our sins?   YES or NO
10. Can Jesus **heal** our bodies?   YES or NO
11. Do you have **faith** in Jesus to forgive you?   YES or NO

WORD LIST

1. **faith** *(noun):* belief in God; believing that God can do great things.
2. **forgiven** *(adjective):* made free from the shame for sin; God choosing to forget our sins.
3. **heal, healed** *(verb):* make well; helped people not be sick any longer.
4. **paralyzed** *(adjective):* cannot move a part of the body; cannot walk or use the hands.
5. **praised** *(verb):* gave thanks to; worshiped; told God how great He is.

6 JESUS CAME TO HELP SINNERS

Memory Verse: ". . . I [Jesus] have not come to call **the righteous**, but **sinners**." (Mark 2:17)
Scripture: Mark 2:15-17

The **Pharisees** (FAIR-uh-seez) were teachers of the laws of the **Jews**. They even made more laws and rules. They **kept** all the laws and rules. They believed that all **Jews** must **keep** the laws and rules too.

Some **Pharisees** thought that they were very holy. They thought that they were holy because they **kept** their laws. They **disliked** the **Jews** who did not **keep** all their laws. Some **Pharisees** even **disliked** Jesus Christ. They thought that He did not **keep** their laws and rules.

One day, Jesus ate a meal at the home of Levi (LEE-vie). Jesus ate with His **disciples** and other people. Some of the other people were **sinners**. The **Pharisees** saw Jesus with the sinners. They asked the **disciples** why Jesus ate with **sinners**.

Jesus said that **sinners** are like sick people. Both **sinners** and sick people need help. Sick people go to doctors for help. But people who are well do not need doctors.

Jesus said that He came to help **sinners**. Jesus can forgive **sinners** of their sins. They need to repent. They need to ask Jesus to forgive them. He can help **sinners** not sin.

The righteous do not need the same help that **sinners** do. Jesus has forgiven them of their sins. **The righteous** love and obey God. They **keep** His laws.

Jesus was not happy with the **Pharisees**. The **Pharisees** said that they loved God. They said that they obeyed God. But the **Pharisees** did not tell the truth.

The **Pharisees** did not love people. The **Pharisees** did not help people. The **Pharisees** did not obey God. They **kept** only their own laws and rules. They thought their laws were better than God's laws.

Today, we should love **sinners**. We should help them know about Jesus. We should help them learn that Jesus will forgive them. We must show them the love of God.

How do you answer these questions? Do you love God? Do you **keep** His laws? Has Jesus forgiven you of your sins? Do you love **sinners**?

QUESTIONS: *Fill in the blanks.*

1. The _____ were teachers of the laws of the **Jews**.
2. Some **Pharisees** thought they were _____ because they **kept** the laws.
3. The **Pharisees** saw _____ eat with **sinners**.
4. Jesus said that He came to help _____.
5. The **Pharisees** did not obey _____.
6. Today, we should love _____ too.

Answer with YES or NO. Circle the right answer.

7. Can Jesus help us not sin?   YES or NO
8. Do **the righteous keep** the laws of God?   YES or NO
9. Was Jesus happy with all the **Pharisees**?   YES or NO
10. Did the **Pharisees** love and help other people?   YES or NO

WORD LIST

1. **disciples** *(noun):* people who follow and obey Jesus Christ. (The 12 men Jesus chose to be His special **disciples**.)
2. **disliked** *(verb):* did not like; did not love.
3. **Jews** *(proper noun):* the people of the country of Israel.
4. **keep, kept** *(verb):* obey; do what the laws and rules say to do.
5. **Pharisees** *(proper noun):* important people in the religion of the Jews; teachers of the laws of the Jews.
6. **sinners** *(noun):* people who sin; people who do not obey the laws of God.
7. **the righteous** *(noun phrase):* good people; people who obey God and His laws; people who do what is right.

7 WE ARE THE FAMILY OF JESUS

Memory Verse: **"Whoever** does **God's will** is My brother and sister and mother." (Mark 3:35)
Scripture: Mark 3:31-35
Background Scripture: Mark 3:1-12, 20-21

Jesus Christ helped many people. They followed Jesus everyplace that He went. They wanted to hear what He said. He often had a crowd near Him.

Jesus did good things for people. He healed sick people. He **encouraged** people. He gave people **hope**.

Jesus taught the people and told them about God. He told them that they could have better lives. He told them about the love of God. This **encouraged** them and gave them **hope**.

Sometimes, the crowd of people would not leave. Jesus could not rest. Sometimes, He could not even eat. But Jesus loved people. He wanted to help them.

One day, Jesus was in a house. His disciples were with Him. Many other people were there too. But all the people did not believe in Jesus. Some people thought that Jesus was sick in His mind.

The mother and brothers of Jesus came to the house. They wanted to see Him. They wanted to take care of Him.

Someone told Jesus that His family was waiting for Him. Jesus said to the people, "You are My family. You are My mother and My brothers. Do **God's will. Whoever** does His will is My brother and sister and mother."

Jesus loved His mother and His brothers. He did not dislike them. He loved everyone. He loves us too. Jesus wants us to know Him. This truth should **encourage** us. This truth should give us **hope**.

We should learn what Jesus taught. We should love and obey God. We should do **God's will**. We should do what God wants. Then, we will be a part of His family.

You can learn about Jesus Christ. You can love Him and obey Him. You can do **God's will**. Then, you can be in His family.

QUESTIONS: *Fill in the blanks.*

1. Jesus Christ_____many people.
2. Jesus often had a_____of people near Him.
3. Jesus told the people about the_____of God.
4. _____ **encouraged** people. He gave them_____.
5. Jesus loved _____. He wanted to help them.
6. We should _____ and _____ God.

Give the answers.

7. What are two ways Jesus helped people?
   (1) He _____ them.
   (2) He _____ them.
8. Who came to get Jesus? His _____
   and _____.
9. What should we do? God's _____.

WORD LIST

1. **encouraged** *(verb):* made people feel better; helped people in their spirits.
2. **God's will** *(noun phrase):* what God wants for all people.
3. **hope** *(noun):* believing that God will do what He says He will do; believing in life after death.
4. **whoever** *(pronoun):* any person; a man, a woman, a young person, or a child.

8   JESUS TAUGHT BY PARABLES

Memory Verse: ". . . hear the **Word of God** and obey it." (Luke 11:28)
Scripture: Mark 4:1-8
Background Scripture: Mark 4:13-20

Large crowds of people followed Jesus. They listened to Him as He taught. Jesus often told stories to the people. We call these stories **parables**.

One day, Jesus told a **parable** about seeds. A farmer planted some seeds to grow food. The farmer threw the seeds on the ground.

Some seeds fell along the path on hard ground. Birds came and ate the seeds quickly. The seeds never did grow.

Some seeds fell on ground with many stones. There was very little soil. The seeds could not grow very well. The new plants died quickly.

Some seeds fell on ground with weeds. The seeds began to grow. But, the weeds kept the good plants from growing very large.

Some seeds fell on good ground. The seeds grew into large plants. The farmer got much food from these plants.

Later, Jesus taught the meaning of the **parable**. The seeds are like the **Word of God**. It can grow like plants grow.

Some people hear the **Word of God**. But Satan takes the **Word of God** away from them. These people are like the hard ground along the path.

Other people hear the **Word of God**. Soon, **trouble** comes to their lives. The people forget the **Word of God**. They turn away from God. These people are like the ground with many stones.

Other people hear the **Word of God**. Later, they begin to **worry** about life. They want many things. They love money and the things that money can buy. They forget the **Word of God**. These people are like the ground with weeds.

Other people hear the **Word of God**. They study the Bible and pray. They ask God to help them. They want to understand the **Word of God**. These people are like the good ground.

Today, people hear the **Word of God**. Some people do not let His Word grow at all. Some people let His Word grow for a little time. **Trouble** comes to them. They **worry** about their lives. Then, they forget about God.

But some people hear the **Word of God**. They remember it. They obey it. These people are happy. These people are like the plants that make good food.

We must hear the **Word of God**. And we must obey it.

QUESTIONS: *Give the answers.*

1. Jesus often told _____ to people. These stories are called _____.
2. Jesus told a **parable** about _____ .
3. The seeds fell on four types of ground. These are:
    (1) _____ ground
    (2) ground with many _____
    (3) ground with _____
    (4) _____ ground
4. The seeds are like the _____ of _____.
5. Today, people _____ the **Word of God**.

Answer with YES or NO. Circle the right answer.

6. Can people hear the **Word of God** today?   YES or NO
7. Do people always remember the **Word of God**?   YES or NO
8. Are people sometimes like the grounds in this **parable**?   YES or NO
9. Is the **Word of God** like the seeds?   YES or NO

WORD LIST

1. **parable, parables** *(noun):* a short story that teaches a lesson. (**Parables** help people understand things about God and the Christian life.)
2. **trouble** *(noun):* problems; temptations; times of hurt and pain.
3. **Word of God** *(proper noun phrase):* the Holy Bible; the truth of God; the law of God.
4. **worry** *(verb):* have no peace in your mind; think about something so much you do not have peace; be afraid of what may happen.

Memory Verse: ". . . He [God] cares for you." (1 Peter 5:7)

9   JESUS STOPPED A STORM

Scripture: Mark 4:35-41

All people are afraid at times. We are afraid of some things. We fear the things that can hurt us. Many people fear storms, and storms make us worry. This lesson is about a bad storm.

Jesus Christ and His disciples were in a boat. They were on Lake Galilee. The lake was **calm**. Jesus was sleeping. **Suddenly**, there was a bad storm. A strong wind blew water into the boat.

The disciples of Jesus were afraid. They were worried. They thought that they would die. They woke Jesus. The disciples asked Him, **"Don't** you care if we **drown**?"

Jesus stood in the boat. He told the wind to stop blowing. **Suddenly**, the wind stopped. The water did not blow into the boat. The lake was **calm** again.

Jesus stopped the storm. He used His great power to stop the wind. He wanted to teach a lesson. Jesus asked His disciples "Why are you so afraid? Why do you worry? **Don't** you have faith in Me?"

Jesus showed His great power in the storm. Jesus showed that He could take care of His disciples. They would not **drown**. He could keep them safe in a storm.

Today, our troubles in life are like storms. Trouble with other people can be like a storm. Money problems can be like a storm. **Sickness** can be like a storm.

Jesus Christ can take care of people today. He can help us in all the "storms of life." He can help us with our problems. We do not have to worry.

Jesus can give us peace in the storms of life. This means that His peace takes away our fear. He gives us peace when we have problems. He gives us peace inside of us. He helps us to be **calm** inside of us. We do not have to be afraid.

We must have faith in Jesus Christ. He will help us in our times of trouble. He will help us to be **calm** inside. He will help us in our **sickness**. Jesus loves us very much. He will take care of us.

QUESTIONS: *Fill in the blanks.*

1. Where were Jesus and His disciples in a boat? On

   _____ _____.

2. What happened **suddenly**? A bad _____.

3. What was Jesus doing when the storm started? He was

   _____.

4. What did Jesus do about the bad storm? He

   _____ it.

5. What can Jesus give us in the storms of life?_____.

6. Who loves us and takes care of us?_____.

Answer YES or NO. Circle the right answer.

7. Did Jesus keep His disciples safe during the storm? YES or NO

8. Can Jesus keep people safe today?   YES or NO

9. Does Jesus want us to be afraid?   YES or NO

10. Do you have faith in Jesus?   YES or NO

WORD LIST

1. **calm** *(adjective):* not moving; quiet; no wind blowing; having peace inside us.
2. **don't** *(contraction):* do not.
3. **drown** *(verb):* die by being under water too long.
4. **sickness** *(noun):* being sick and feeling bad; not well in our bodies.
5. **suddenly** *(adverb):* very fast; quickly.

10 JESUS HAD POWER OVER AN EVIL SPIRIT

Memory Verse: "... be strong in the Lord and in His **mighty** power." (Ephesians 6:10)
Scripture: Mark 5:1-8
Background Scripture: Mark 5:9-20

Jesus Christ went across Lake Galilee in a boat. A man came to Jesus. This man had an **evil spirit** or a **demon**. This **evil spirit** caused the man many problems.

The man did strange things. He yelled and shouted. He cut his own body with stones. He did not wear clothes. People were afraid to go near him.

Jesus loved this man. Jesus wanted to help him. Jesus knew a **demon** made the man do strange things.

The **demon** knew that Jesus was the Son of God. The **demon** knew Jesus had **mighty** power. Jesus talked to the **demon**. Jesus said, "Come out of this man!"

Jesus asked the **evil spirit**, "What is your name?" The **evil spirit** answered, "Many." He meant that there were lots of **evil spirits** in the man.

Then, the **evil spirits** came out of the man. They went into 2,000 pigs. The pigs ran into a lake. The pigs drowned.

The man was well after the **demon** left him. He put on clothes. He was quiet. He did not do strange things any more.

Jesus showed His **mighty** power over the **evil spirit**. He showed His **mighty** power to heal the man. Jesus showed His power to **overcome** the power of Satan.

Soon, it was time for Jesus to leave that place. The man asked Jesus, "May I go with you?" Jesus answered, "No. Go home to your family. Tell them how much the Lord has done for you."

The man obeyed and went away. He told everyone what Jesus had done. He **witnessed** about the **mighty** power of God.

Today, God still has power over **demons**. God is stronger than all evil. He wants to help us with our problems. He will help us **overcome** evil. He will help us **overcome** sin.

We should tell other people when God helps us. All people need to know about the **mighty** power of God. We should **witness** for God. He loves everyone. He wants to help them too.

QUESTIONS: *Fill in the blanks.*

1. The man had an _____ _____.
2. The **demon** caused the man many_____.
3. Jesus said to the **demon**, "Come _____ of this man!"
4. Jesus showed His **mighty** _____ over the **evil spirit**.
5. The man was_____after the **demon** left him.
6. God will help us_____evil and sin.

Give the answers.

7. What was the name of the **demon**?_____.
8. Who has power over **demons**?_____.
9. Who is stronger than all evil?_____.
10. What should we do when God helps us?_____.

WORD LIST

1. **demon, demons** *(noun):* an evil spirit; a bad spirit that works against God and for Satan.
2. **evil spirit, evil spirits** *(noun phrase):* a **demon**; bad spirits that work against God and for Satan.
3. **mighty** *(adjective):* great; very strong; with much power.
4. **overcome** *(verb):* be stronger than; have more power than; to win.
5. **witness, witnessed** *(verb):* tell people what God has done for you; tell people about Jesus Christ.

11 JESUS HAD POWER OVER DEATH

Memory Verse: ". . . whoever believes in Him [Jesus] shall . . . have
eternal life." (John 3:16)
Scripture: Mark 5:21-24, 35-43

One day, many people came to see Jesus. A man named Jairus (JAY-rus) was in the crowd. Jairus was an important man. He was a **ruler** in the **synagogue**.

Jairus had a **daughter**. She was very sick. Jairus was an important **ruler** in the **synagogue**. But he could not help her. Yet, he believed that Jesus could help her. He had faith in Jesus.

Jairus went to Jesus. Jairus said, "My **daughter** is dying. I know You can heal her. Please come to my house."

Jesus started to the house of Jairus. On the way, some men came to Jesus and Jairus. The men said to Jairus, "Your **daughter** is dead. Jesus does not need to come to your house." But Jesus went with Jairus anyway.

Everyone in the house of Jairus was sad. They were crying. Jesus said to them, "Don't cry. The girl is not dead. She is sleeping."

The people laughed at Jesus. They knew the **daughter** of Jairus was dead. They did not believe Jesus. They did not believe in His mighty power. They did not have faith as Jairus had.

Jesus knew that the people did not believe Him. Jesus knew that they did not have faith in Him. He wanted them to see the power of God.

Jesus told everyone to leave the house. Only the parents and His disciples stayed with Him. He held the hand of the dead girl. Jesus told her to stand. Then the **daughter** of Jairus stood up and walked. She was alive again! This was a great miracle.

Today, many people are afraid to die. They do not know what happens after death. The Bible tells us what happens after death.

The Bible says sinners go to **hell** after they die. **Hell** is a very bad place. Sinners will never leave **hell**. God punishes them for their sins in **hell forever**.

The Bible says that Christians go to heaven after they die.

Heaven is a happy place. No person is sad in heaven. There is no sickness in heaven. Christians want to go to heaven. Christians should not be afraid to die.

Are you afraid to die? Do you know where you will go after you die? You can know. Believe in Jesus Christ. He will give you **eternal life**. You will live in heaven **forever**.

QUESTIONS: *Fill in the blanks.*

1. The _____ of Jairus was sick, and she died.
2. Jairus had _____ in Jesus.
3. Jesus used His mighty _____ to heal the **daughter** of Jairus. She was _____ again!

Give the answers.

4. Where do sinners go after they die?_____.
5. Where do Christians go after they die?_____.
6. Whom must we believe in to have **eternal life forever?**_____.

Answer with YES or NO. Circle the right answer.

7. Is **hell** a nice place to go to?   YES or NO
8. Will sinners go to heaven?   YES or NO
9. Do Christians believe that they live after death?   YES or NO
10. Should Christians be afraid to die?   YES or NO

WORD LIST

1. **daughter** *(noun):* a girl child of a mother and father.
2. **eternal life** *(noun phrase):* the life that God gives; the life with God now and life with God **forever** in heaven.
3. **forever** *(adverb):* time that has no end; time that goes on and on and on.
4. **hell** *(noun):* the home of sinners after they die; a place where God punishes people **forever** for their sins.
5. **ruler** *(noun):* a person who leads other people; a person who writes rules or laws.
6. **synagogue** *(noun):* a place of worship for the Jews; a church.

12 JESUS GAVE COURAGE

Memory Verse: "... **Take courage**! It is I [Jesus]. Don't be afraid."
   (Mark 6:50)
Scripture: Mark 6:45-51

Jesus Christ is **powerful**. Jesus does things that people cannot do. Jesus is the Son of God. We can trust Jesus. He does not want us to be afraid.

Jesus taught His disciples to trust Him. The disciples saw Him do things that **amazed** them. They saw the mighty power of God in Jesus. They saw the miracles that He did.

One time, Jesus sent His disciples to the town of Bethsaida (beth-SAY-uh-duh). They went in a boat across a lake. Then, Jesus went up on a mountain. He wanted to be alone. He wanted to pray to God.

Later, there was a wind storm. The wind blew and blew and blew. The wind was very strong and **powerful**. The disciples had trouble with their boat. They were afraid that they might drown.

Jesus saw the boat in the storm. He went to the disciples. He walked across the water. The disciples thought Jesus was a **ghost**. The disciples were more afraid.

Jesus spoke to the disciples. He said, "**Take courage**. It is I. Don't be afraid." Then, the disciples knew it was Jesus. He was not a **ghost**. He got into the boat. The storm suddenly stopped.

Jesus **amazed** His disciples. He walked on the water. He stopped the wind storm. This was another miracle.

Jesus showed the disciples that they could trust Him. He showed that He cared for them. Jesus showed that He was **powerful**. He showed that He had power over the wind. He had power over all things.

Jesus also gave **courage** to His disciples. He helped them not be afraid.

Today, Jesus will give us **courage**. He will help us in our troubles. He will help us when we are afraid. He will help us with His mighty power. He will **amaze** us with His power.

Some people are afraid to talk to new people. Some people are afraid to start a new job. Some people are afraid to witness for God. But Jesus knows our fears. We can pray to Him for help. He will give us **courage**.

QUESTIONS: *Fill in the blanks.*

1. Jesus is _____.
   He does things that people cannot do.
2. Jesus does not want us to be_____.
3. Jesus showed the disciples that they could_____Him.
4. Jesus had power over all_____.
5. Jesus gave_____to His disciples.
6. Today, Jesus will help us when we are_____.

Answer with YES or NO. Circle the right answer.

7. Is Jesus the Son of God?   YES or NO
8. Does Jesus have power over wind and water?   YES or NO
9. Does Jesus want us to be afraid?   YES or NO
10. Do you believe Jesus can give you **courage**?   YES or NO

WORD LIST

1. **amaze, amazed** *(verb):* to surprise in a great way; did something that is hard to understand.
2. **courage** *(noun):* not be afraid; being strong inside of you when you are afraid; being strong inside when you have troubles.
3. **ghost** *(noun):* the spirit of a dead person.
4. **powerful** *(adjective):* with much power; able to do great things.
5. **take courage** *(verb phrase):* do not be afraid; have **courage**.

13 JESUS TAUGHT ABOUT OBEYING GOD

Memory Verse: "If you love Me, keep my commands." (John 14:15)
Scripture: Mark 7:1-8
Background Scripture: Mark 7:9-13, 20-23

God gave His laws to the Jews. God gave 10 important laws to them. We call these laws the **Ten Commandments**. You can read about the **Ten Commandments** in the Bible. See Exodus 20:1-17. God **commanded** the people to obey His laws.

The Pharisees made more laws. These laws were not the laws of God. These laws were the laws of people. The Jews had one law about washing hands. They had to wash their hands in a special way. Then they could eat a meal.

One day, the disciples of Jesus were eating. They had not washed their hands in the special way. The Pharisees saw that the disciples had not washed their hands. The Pharisees disliked this. They told Jesus that His disciples had **disobeyed** the law.

Jesus told the Pharisees that they were wrong. The Pharisees were not thinking about the **Ten Commandments**. They were only thinking about their own laws. Jesus told them that they did not honor their parents. Jesus meant that they did not take care of their parents.

God **commanded**, "Honor your father and your mother . . . " (Exodus 20:12) This is one of the **Ten Commandments**. But the Pharisees said, "We give our money to the church. We do not have to take care of our parents." Jesus said the Pharisees **disobeyed** this law of God.

Today, God does not judge us by what we eat. He does not judge us by how we wash our hands. God judges us by how we obey Him. He wants us to obey His laws **rather than** the laws of people. He wants us to obey Him because we love Him.

Sin comes from inside of us. Our evil thoughts are sin. Our wrong acts are sin. But our wrong acts begin in our minds. Jesus said that all evil begins inside us.

God wants us to be clean. But He wants us to be clean on the inside. He wants to free us from sin. Only Jesus has the power to take away our sins. Only Jesus can make us clean inside. Only

Jesus can be our **Savior** (SAYV-yer).

We are clean inside when we **accept** Jesus as our **Savior**. We are clean inside as we obey God. We sin when we **disobey** God. Are you clean inside? Have you **accepted** Jesus as your **Savior**?

QUESTIONS: *Give the answers.*

1. What were the ten important laws called? The_____
   _____.
2. What did the Pharisees say about the disciples of Jesus? They had_____the law.
3. How does God judge us? By how we_____Him.
4. What comes from inside of us?_____.
5. Who has the power to make us clean inside?_____.

Answer with YES or NO. Circle the right answers.

6. Were the laws made by the Pharisees the laws
   of God?   YES or NO
7. Did the Pharisees honor their parents?   YES or NO
8. Are our wrong acts sins?   YES or NO
9. Can Jesus save you from sin?   YES or NO
10. Have you **accepted** Jesus as your **Savior**?   YES or NO

WORD LIST

1. **accept, accepted** *(verb):* agree to receive; agree in your mind and heart.
2. **command, commands, commanded** *(verb):* tell someone to do something; told someone to obey.
3. **disobey, disobeyed** *(verb):* did not obey; did not do what God told them to do.
4. **rather than** *(prepositional phrase):* instead of, in place of.
5. **Savior** *(proper noun):* Jesus Christ; the Son of God; the One who came to save people from their sins and hell.
6. **Ten Commandments** *(proper noun phrase):* important laws that God gave to the Jews through Moses.

14 JESUS FED A LARGE CROWD

Memory Verse: ". . . God will **meet all your needs** . . ." (Philippians 4:19)

Scripture: Mark 8:1-10

One time, Jesus taught a large crowd of people. There were 4,000 men in the crowd. They had been with Jesus for three days. The people had no food, and they were hungry.

Jesus was sad. He wanted the people to eat. Jesus did not want the people to go home hungry. They could become sick.

The disciples of Jesus did not have much food. They did not have any **extra** food. They could not buy any more food. They did not have enough money. And there was no town near to them.

Jesus asked, "How much bread do you have?" The disciples answered, "We have seven **loaves** of bread."

Jesus told the people to sit down. He thanked God for the food. Then, He broke the **loaves** of bread into pieces. The disciples gave the bread to the people.

They also had some small fish. Jesus thanked God for the fish. He broke the fish into pieces. The disciples gave the fish to the people.

There was much food. The people could not eat all the food. The disciples picked up the **extra** food. This was a miracle. Once again, Jesus used His mighty power to help people.

Jesus fed the large crowd. Then, He sent the people away. The people were not hungry any longer. They could go home and not get sick.

Today, Jesus knows everything that we need. We may be hungry. We may need a job or clothes. We may need friends. We may need someone to help us. We can pray and ask Jesus for what we need.

Jesus is kind, and He loves us very much. He wants to help us. He wants to **meet all our needs**. The Bible says, "God will **meet all your needs**." See the memory verse.

Jesus can do miracles in our lives today. But we must believe in Him. We must have faith in Him. We must believe that He is the Son of God.

QUESTIONS: *Fill in the blanks.*

1. The people had no_____, and they were very hungry.
2. Jesus was _____. He wanted the people to
   _____ before they went home.
3. Jesus _____ God for the food.
4. Jesus is _____, and He_____us very much.
5. Jesus can do_____in our lives today.

Give the answers.

6. How many men were in the crowd of people?_____.
7. How many **loaves** of bread did the disciples have?_____.
8. Who ate the food and were not hungry?_____.
9. Who will **meet all our needs?**_____.
10. To whom can we pray and ask for what we need?_____.

WORD LIST

1. **extra** *(adjective):* more than is needed; more than enough.
2. **loaves** *(noun):* more than one loaf of bread. (A loaf is a large
   piece of bread before it is cut into smaller pieces.)
3. **meet all your needs, meet all our needs** *(verb phrase):* give you
   everything that you need; do for you everything that needs
   to be done.

15 JESUS TAUGHT ABOUT FOLLOWING HIM

Memory Verse: ". . . **take up [your] cross** and follow Me." (Mark 8:34)
Scripture: Mark 8:34-38

Jesus was going to another city. He taught His disciples as they went. Jesus saw many people along the road. He taught them with His disciples.

Jesus said, "You may want to follow Me. But you must say 'no' to anything that **separates** you from God."

Jesus also commanded, "You must obey the Word of God. You must say 'yes' to the will of God. You may have to **suffer** for Me. You may have to die for your faith in Me."

Jesus also taught, "Anyone who gives his life to Me will live forever. Anyone who believes the good news will live forever. You can have many things and much money. But if you do not follow Me, you have nothing. You will not go to heaven."

Today, we live in a world full of sin. Many people live only for things that they want. They don't think of other people. They only want to have a fun time. They do things that hurt their bodies. These people do not give their lives to God.

Some people are afraid to follow Jesus. They think that they may have to **suffer**. Jesus is not happy with these people. He said these people are not His children. They will not go to heaven when they die.

Some people know how to follow Jesus. They have learned what Jesus taught. They know when to say "no." They say "no" to anything that **separates** them from God. And they say "yes" to what God wants.

Jesus **suffered** and died for us. He died on the **Cross** to save us from sin. God wanted to save us from sin. That is why God sent Jesus to earth. And Jesus obeyed God.

Today, most of us will not die on a **cross**. But Jesus said we must **take up our cross**. This means that we must say "no" to what we want. We must say "no" to anything that **separates** us from God. We must say "yes" to following Jesus.

Sometimes, this is hard to do. Yet, we must choose to follow Jesus. We must accept Jesus as our Savior. We must obey God and His laws. We must **take up our cross**. Then, we will have eternal life with God forever.

QUESTIONS: *Fill in the blanks.*

1. Jesus said, ". . . **take up your cross** and_____Me."
2. Jesus said we must say "_____" to the will of God.
3. Anyone who gives his life to Jesus will live_____.
4. We must say "no" to anything that_____us from God.
5. We must accept Jesus as our_____to have eternal life.

Answer with YES or NO. Circle the right answer.

6. Will people go to heaven who don't follow Jesus? YES or NO
7. Do we live in a world full of sin?   YES or NO
8. Did Jesus die on the **Cross** to save us from sin?   YES or NO
9. Today, will most people die on a **cross**?   YES or NO
10. Is it easy to **take up our cross** and follow Jesus?   YES or NO

WORD LIST

1. **cross** *(noun)*, **Cross** *(proper noun):* a tool, made of two pieces of wood, used for killing people; usually has the shape of the letter T. (Jesus died by hanging on a **cross**.)
2. **separates** *(verb):* not together; keeps away from.
3. **suffer, suffered** *(verb):* have pain; hurt; do without things you think you need.
4. **take up your cross, take up our cross** *(verb phrase):* follow Jesus; obey God; do everything God wants you to do.

16 JESUS TAUGHT ABOUT SERVING OTHER PEOPLE

Memory Verse: "... serve one another humbly in love." (Galatians 5:13)
Scripture: Mark 9:30-35

One day, Jesus took His disciples away from the crowd. He did not want the crowd to know where they were. He wanted to be alone with His disciples. He wanted to teach them.

Jesus told them what would happen to Him. He said that some men would kill Him. But He would live again. Jesus **predicted** His own death and **resurrection**. The disciples did not know what Jesus meant. And they were afraid to ask Him any questions.

Jesus and His disciples were going to Capernaum (kuh-PER-nee-um). Jesus heard the disciples talking. They were **arguing** with each other.

They came to the city of Capernaum. They went inside a house. Jesus asked, "What were you **arguing** about?" The disciples did not answer Jesus. They knew that they were wrong. They had **argued** about who was the most important disciple.

Jesus sat down. He called the 12 disciples to Him. He talked to them about being **selfish**. He talked to them about their wrong thoughts and words.

Jesus said that everyone likes to be **first**. But every person cannot always be **first**. Sometimes, a person must be **last**. He or she must be a **servant**. This means that he or she must serve other people.

Jesus was a **servant**. He showed us how to serve other people. He did not come to earth to be **first**. Jesus came to be a **servant** of all people. He was not **selfish**. He came to die for our sins.

Today, we should be like Jesus. We should be willing to serve other people. We should help people when they need our help. We should do good things for people. We should not be **selfish**.

There are many ways that we can serve people. One important way is to witness for Jesus. We should tell other people what Jesus has done for us. We should tell people about Jesus' death and **resurrection**.

We need to serve people in the ways we can. God will help us to be good **servants**. He will help us to be **last**. Then, we will be **first**. God loves us very much. He wants us to love and serve Him.

QUESTIONS: *Fill in the blanks.*

1. Jesus_____His own death and **resurrection**.
2. The disciples_____about who was the most important disciple.
3. Jesus said the disciples were_____.
4. People like to be_____, but we cannot always be **first**.
5. Sometimes, a person must be_____. This means that we must serve_____.
6. Jesus was a_____. He showed us how to_____ other people.

Give the answers.

7. What did Jesus **predict**? His own_____ and_____.
8. How was Jesus a **servant**? He came to_____ for our_____.
9. Whom should we be like today?_____.
10. What is one important way to serve other people?_____
_____.

WORD LIST

1. **argued, arguing** *(verb):* fighting with words; not agreeing with.
2. **first** *(adjective):* very important; the most important person.
3. **last** *(adjective):* not very important; the least important person.
4. **predict, predicted** *(verb):* tell what is going to happen before it happens.
5. **resurrection** *(noun):* living again after death; coming back to life after dying.
6. **selfish** *(adjective):* thinking only of your own self; not thinking about other people.
7. **servant, servants** *(noun):* a person who works for or serves other people.

17 JESUS TAUGHT ABOUT ETERNAL LIFE

Memory Verse: ". . . the gift of God is eternal life in Christ Jesus our Lord." (Romans 6:23)
Scripture: Mark 10:17-27

One day, a young man ran to Jesus. The young man was rich. He asked Jesus how to get eternal life.

Jesus told the man to obey the laws of God. Jesus said, "You must not kill people. You must not do sex sins. You must not steal or lie. You must honor your mother and father. You must obey all the laws of God."

The man said that he had obeyed all those laws. But he felt he must do something more. He felt that he must **earn** eternal life.

Jesus loved the young man. But Jesus knew the man loved money. Jesus wanted the man to love Him more than money. Jesus told him, "Sell everything you have. Give the money to the poor. Follow Me. Then, you will have eternal life."

The young man was very sad. He had much money. He wanted to keep his money. He walked away from Jesus. The words of Jesus were **difficult** for the young man to understand. He did not obey Jesus.

Jesus spoke to His disciples. "It is **difficult** for a rich man to follow Me." Jesus meant that a person must love Him more than money. A person must love Jesus most of all.

The words of Jesus amazed the disciples. They asked, "Who then can be **saved**?" They thought eternal life was **impossible** for some people.

Jesus answered, "Everyone can be **saved**. Eternal life is **impossible** with man. But, eternal life is **possible** with God. All things are **possible** with God."

Today, rich people can have eternal life. They can be **saved** too. But they must love God more than their money. Money is not wrong. But the love of money is wrong. Money must not be the most important thing to us. God must be most important in our lives.

We must be willing to follow Jesus. We must be willing to give our money to God. We must be willing to obey Jesus. We must accept Jesus as our Savior. Then we can be **saved**. We can have eternal life. We cannot **earn** it. Eternal life is the gift of God to us.

QUESTIONS: *Fill in the blanks.*

1. The young man was _____.
2. The man wanted to know how to get _____

   _____.
3. The young man obeyed all the_____of God.
4. Jesus told the man to_____everything he had.
5. It is_____for a rich man to follow Jesus.
6. We must be_____to obey Jesus.

Give the answers.

7. Whom must we love most of all?_____.
8. What is **possible** with God?_____.
9. What is the gift of God to us?_____.

Answer with YES or NO. Circle the right answer.

10. Are all things **possible** with God?   YES or NO
11. Can we **earn** eternal life?   YES or NO
12. Are you **saved**?   YES or NO

WORD LIST

1. **difficult** *(adjective):* not easy; hard to do.
2. **earn** *(verb):* work for; do something to get something else.
3. **impossible** *(adjective):* not **possible**; cannot happen; not able to be done.
4. **possible** *(adjective):* may happen; may be done.
5. **saved** *(verb):* have eternal life; will not be punished in hell for sin.

18 PEOPLE PRAISED JESUS CHRIST

Memory Verse: "Praise the Lord . . ." (Psalm 150:1)
Scripture: Mark 11:1-11

Jesus Christ taught His disciples for about three years. He had told the disciples about His death. But they did not believe He would die.

Jesus and His disciples were going to the city of Jerusalem (juh-REW-suh-lum). Jesus sent two disciples to find a **colt**. He said, "Go to the next town. You will find a **colt** there. Bring it to me."

The disciples found the **colt**. Jesus rode the **colt** into Jerusalem. The people sang songs of praise to Jesus. They shouted, "**Hosanna!** Jesus is the One who comes in the name of the Lord!" The friends of Jesus felt very happy.

Other people put their coats on the road. Some people put **palm** branches on the road. Many people waved **palm** branches and shouted, "**Hosanna!**" These acts showed love for Jesus.

The people thought that Jesus would be their king on earth. They were wrong. Jesus wanted to be King of their lives. He wanted to **rule** their lives.

Today, Jesus wants to be the King of our lives. He wants to **rule** our lives. He wants us to worship Him as King.

Today, we remember the day Jesus rode into Jerusalem. We call this day **Palm Sunday**. Christians give special honor to Jesus Christ on **Palm Sunday**. We praise the Son of God. We worship Him as King of our lives.

We need to praise God. We need to praise Him every day. We need to praise God for His love for us. We need to praise Him for Jesus Christ, our Savior.

The Psalms are good for us to read. The Psalms praise God. The memory verse says, "Praise the Lord." Look at the last five psalms. Each one begins and ends with "Praise the Lord."

"Praise the Lord!" This is a good verse for us to remember. We should say it every day. The Lord is our God! He is King of our lives!

QUESTIONS: *Fill in the blanks.*

1. Jesus Christ taught people for about_____years.
2. Jesus was on His way to_____.
3. Jesus rode into Jerusalem on a_____.
4. The people sang songs of_____to Jesus.
5. Jesus wants to be_____of our_____.
6. The_____are good to read because they praise God.
7. The memory verse says, "_____
   _____ _____."

Answer YES or NO. Circle the right answer.

8. Did the people think Jesus would be their king on earth?   YES or NO
9. Did Jesus want to be a king on earth?   YES or NO
10. Do we remember **Palm Sunday** because Jesus died on this day?   YES or NO
11. Should we praise God only once a year?   YES or NO
12. Does Jesus Christ **rule** your life?   YES or NO

WORD LIST

1. **colt** *(noun):* a young horse.
2. **hosanna** (hoh-ZAH-nuh) *(noun):* "save" or "save us"; a word used to show praise to Jesus Christ.
3. **palm** *(noun):* a type of tree. (**Palm** trees grow where the weather is warm all year.)
4. **Palm Sunday** *(proper noun phrase):* the Sunday before Easter; the special day Christians remember Jesus riding a **colt** into Jerusalem.
5. **rule** *(verb):* control; be in charge of our lives.

19 JESUS TAUGHT ABOUT LOVING GOD

Memory Verse: "Love the Lord your God with all your heart . . . **soul** . . . mind and . . . **strength**." (Mark 12:30)
Scripture: Mark 12:28-34

One day, some teachers of the law came to Jesus. They asked Him some questions. They wanted to know about the laws of God. Jesus gave them good answers. One man asked Jesus which law was the most important.

Jesus said, "You must love God more than anything else. You must love God with all your heart and **soul**. You must love God with all your mind and **strength**. This is the most important law of all."

Then Jesus said, "You must love your **neighbors**. You must love them as much as **yourself**. This law is the second most important law. No other laws are more important than these two laws."

Today, we should ask and answer these questions. How much do I love God? Is God most important to me? Is He first in my life? Do I love my **neighbors** as I love **myself**?

We must do more than say "I love God." We must believe He is the one and only God. We must believe in Him with our minds and hearts. We must worship Him. We must praise Him. God must be most important to us.

We must show that we love God. The way we act shows our love for God. We must obey His laws. We must do what Jesus taught us to do. We must love Him with all our **strength**.

Then, we must love our **neighbors** as ourselves. We can help our **neighbors** when they need help. We can share with them what we have. We can help them when they are sick.

We also help people when we witness to them. We witness by telling our **neighbors** about Jesus. We witness when we help our **neighbors**. We show them the love of God by our kind acts. We witness when we love our **neighbors** as ourselves.

Can you say, "I love God with my heart, **soul**, mind, and **strength**?" Can you say, "I love my **neighbors** as I love **myself**?" God must be most important of all. Other people must be important to us too. Then, we obey what Jesus taught about loving God.

QUESTIONS: *Fill in the blanks.*

1. One man asked Jesus which _____ of God was most important.

2. Jesus said, "You must _____ _____ more than anything else."

3. "You must love your _____ as **yourself**."

4. We help people when we _____ to them.

5. We show our **neighbors** the love of God by our _____ _____.

6. The memory verse says, "Love the Lord your God with all your _____ . . . _____ . . . _____ and . . . _____ ."

Give the answers.

7. Whom should we worship and praise?_____.

8. Who must be most important of all?_____.

9. Whom must we love as ourselves?_____.

WORD LIST

1. **myself** *(pronoun):* me; the same person as I.
2. **neighbors** *(noun):* people living near you. (In this lesson, neighbors can also mean any people.)
3. **soul** *(noun):* the part of the person that lives after death.
4. **strength** *(noun):* being strong in your spirit; having power inside of you.
5. **yourself** *(pronoun):* you; the same person as you.

20 JESUS TAUGHT ABOUT SUFFERING

Memory Verse: ". . . the one who **stands firm** to the end will be
   saved." (Mark 13:13)
Scripture: Mark 13:7-9, 13
Background Scripture: Mark 13:1-6, 8-12

One day, Jesus was on the Mount of Olives (AHL-ivz). Peter,
James, John, and Andrew were with Him. Jesus talked with His
disciples about the end of the earth. They asked Him, "When will
this happen?"

Jesus said that there will be many troubles. The end of the earth
will come after the troubles. He said that there will be many wars.
Nations will fight other nations. The earth will not have peace.

Jesus said that there would be **earthquakes** and **famines**. The
earth will shake with great **earthquakes**. Buildings will fall down.
People will be hurt and die. There will be **famines** too. There will be
no food. People will be sick and die from being hungry.

Jesus said to the disciples, "Watch out. Evil people will come
to get you. They will hit you in places of worship. You will have
suffering because of Me. You will have to stand before kings and
other **leaders**. You will be there to tell them about Me."

Jesus said, "All people will hate you. They will hate you because
you follow Me. But you will be saved if you are **true** to Me. You
must **stand firm** before people, kings, and other **leaders**. You must
be **true** to Me until the end."

Jesus told the disciples about these things that would happen.
He told them to **expect** troubles. His **followers** would have **suffering**
because of Him.

Today, life is not always easy for Christians. People who follow
Jesus may **expect** problems. They may **expect suffering**. Sometimes,
bad things happen to good people.

But Jesus wants His **followers** to be **true** to Him. Jesus promises
to help them. He also promises that they will be saved. Jesus will
reward His **followers** for being **true** to Him. The reward is eternal
life.

Jesus is our friend. He will help us in our **suffering**. He will give us
strength. He will help us **stand firm**. Then, we will be saved at the
end of our lives. This is a promise from our Lord.

QUESTIONS: *Fill in the blanks.*

1. Jesus said there would be many _____
   before the end of the earth.

2. Jesus said to the disciples, "All people will _____ you.
   They will hate you because you _____ Me."

3. Life is not always _____ for Christians.

4. Jesus wants His **followers** to be _____ to Him.

5. Jesus is our _____. He will
   help us in our _____.

6. People who **stand firm** to the end will be _____.

Answer with YES or NO. Circle the right answer.

7. Will Christians be saved if they are **true** to Jesus?   YES or NO
8. Can Christians **expect** problems?   YES or NO
9. Will Christians never have problems in life?   YES or NO
10. Does Jesus help you in your **suffering**?   YES or NO

WORD LIST

1. **earthquakes** *(noun):* the earth or ground shaking and moving.
2. **expect** *(verb):* think something will happen.
3. **famines** *(noun):* times when there is little or no food; times
   when people are sick or die because they are hungry.
4. **followers** *(noun):* Christians; people who believe in Jesus Christ
   and follow Him; people who obey what Jesus taught.
5. **leaders** *(noun):* people who lead or rule other people. (**Leaders**
   are sometimes rulers of nations or groups of people.)
6. **stand firm, stands firm** *(verb phrase):* does not stop believing
   in God; is true to God.
7. **suffering** *(noun):* having troubles, pain, and hurt in life.
8. **true** *(adjective):* loyal. (In this lesson, **true** means to follow
   Jesus always. To be **true** means to love and obey Jesus.)

21 JESUS WILL COME AGAIN

Memory Verse: "... I [Jesus] will **come back** ..." (John 14:3)
Scripture: Mark 13:24-27, 32-33

Jesus was on the Mount of Olives. He was talking to four of His disciples. He was talking about the end of the earth. He was telling them about things that will happen.

Jesus said that days of trouble will come first. Then, **terrible** things will happen in the sky. The sun will not shine. The moon will not shine. The stars will fall out of the sky. People will then know the end will come soon.

Next, everyone will see the Son of Man coming. He will come in the clouds. He will come with power and **glory**. His angels will be with Him.

Jesus will send His angels to find Christians. They will go around the earth. They will bring all saved people to Him.

Jesus said that no person knows when this will happen. No one knows the day. The angels do not know. Even Jesus does not know. Only God, the Father, knows.

Jesus told His disciples, "Watch for Me! Always be ready! You do not know when the time will come."

Today, Christians believe that Jesus is coming again. We believe He is coming in power and **glory**. We believe that He is coming **for sure**. We are watching for Jesus. We know **terrible** things will happen first. Then He will **come back.**

But we do not know when Jesus will **come back.** It may be today. It may be next year. It may be many years from now. Yet, He is coming **for sure** in power and **glory**.

We must be ready for Jesus to **come back.** We cannot get ready after He comes. It will be too late then. We must get ready now.

How can we get ready? We must become Christians. We must believe that Jesus is the Son of God. We must believe that He died for sins. We must ask Jesus to forgive our sins. We must turn from our sins. We must accept Jesus as our Savior.

Then, we must study the Holy Bible. We must obey the Word of God. We must obey what Jesus taught. We must learn how to live a Christian life. We must grow as Christians.

Jesus is coming again **for sure**. Are you ready? You can be ready now.

QUESTIONS: *Fill in the blanks.*

1. Jesus said that He will_____.
   (See memory verse.)
2. _____things will happen in the
   sky before Jesus **comes back**.
3. Jesus will send His angels all over the earth. They will bring all
   _____to Him.
4. Only_____knows when Jesus will **come back**.
5. We must be_____for Jesus. It will be too
   _____after He **comes back**.
6. We must be a_____to be ready for Jesus. We
   must accept_____as our_____.

Answer with YES or NO. Circle the right answer.

7. Does the Bible say when Jesus will **come back**?   YES or NO
8. Can you get ready after Jesus **comes back**?   YES or NO
9. Can every person be ready for Jesus to come?   YES or NO
10. Are you ready for Jesus to **come back**?   YES or NO

WORD LIST

1. **come back** *(verb phrase):* return; come again. (In this lesson,
   come back means that Jesus will return to earth.)
2. **for sure** *(prepositional phrase):* for certain; something that will
   happen.
3. **glory** *(noun):* a word that tells us about God. (**Glory** means
   how great and important God is.)
4. **terrible** *(adjective):* very, very bad; causing great fear.

22 A WOMAN GAVE JESUS A SPECIAL GIFT

Memory Verse: "We love because He [Jesus] first loved us." (1 John 4:19)

Scripture: Mark 14:1-9

Jesus Christ was in Bethany (BETH-uh-nee). Bethany was a small town near Jerusalem. Jesus was at the house of a friend. The name of His friend was Simon (SIE-mun). Jesus and His friends were eating and resting.

A woman was in Bethany too. She came into the house of Simon. She carried an **alabaster** jar. **Perfume** was in the jar. This **perfume** cost much money.

The woman went to Jesus. She broke the **alabaster** jar. She poured the **perfume** on His head. She did a **beautiful** thing. She gave **beautiful service** to Jesus.

Some of the people who saw her were angry. They thought the woman should not have done this. They thought the woman should sell the **perfume**. Then, the money could buy food for poor people.

These people were not kind to the woman. They told her that she did a bad thing. They did not think her **service** was **beautiful**.

"Leave her alone," said Jesus. "She has done a **beautiful** thing to Me. There will always be poor people. You can help them anytime."

Jesus knew that He would die soon. His friends would put His body in a **tomb**. Jesus said, "This woman did what she could. She put **perfume** on My body. She has made Me ready for the **tomb**."

The **perfume** cost much money. But, the woman loved Jesus very much. The **perfume** was her special gift to Jesus. Her gift was a gift of true love.

Jesus liked her gift of love. He said, "People will always remember this woman. People will remember her for what she has done. They will remember her **beautiful service** to Me."

Today we love our families and friends. We love the things we own. But we must love Jesus more than people and things. We must love Jesus most of all.

We can give Jesus a special gift also. We can give Him our praise and worship. We can give Him our love. We can give Jesus our lives. We can give Him our **service**. Our **service** can be **beautiful** too.

QUESTIONS: *Fill in the blanks.*

1. Jesus was in the house of His friend named_____.
2. A woman poured_____on the head of Jesus.
3. Jesus said, "This woman has done a_____thing."
4. Jesus also said, "This woman has made Me ready for the _____."
5. The woman gave Jesus a gift of true_____.
6. We must love_____most of all.
7. We must love Jesus more than our_____and _____.

Give the answers.

8. Where was Jesus?_____.
9. Why were the people angry with the woman? Because they said the woman should sell the_____ and use the money to buy_____for poor people.
10. What are two special gifts you can give to Jesus?
    (1)_____.
    (2)_____.

WORD LIST

1. **alabaster** (AL-uh-BAS-ter) *(adjective):* a type of stone used to make pretty jars and other things.
2. **beautiful** *(adjective):* very good; very kind; very nice.
3. **perfume** *(noun):* something that has a nice smell. (People put perfume on their bodies to make them smell nice.)
4. **service** *(noun):* what people do to serve Jesus; all the things people do to help Jesus on earth.
5. **tomb** *(noun):* a place where we put a dead person.

23 JESUS ATE THE PASSOVER MEAL

Memory Verse: "... do this **in remembrance of** Me." (Luke 22:19)
Scripture: Mark 14:12-15, 22-25
Background Scripture: Luke 22:7-20

The Jews have a special meal once a year. They call this meal the **Passover** meal. All Jews eat this meal. The Jews remember how God helped them to leave Egypt (EE-jipt). Egypt is a country near Israel (IZ-ree-ul).

Jesus ate the **Passover** meal each year. It was time for the **Passover** once again. Jesus sent two of His disciples to the city. He told them to get the meal ready.

Jesus knew that this **Passover** was His last one. He knew that He would soon die. Jesus wanted His disciples to remember Him after He was gone. He wanted them to know what His death meant.

Jesus talked about His death during the **Passover** meal. He broke some bread into pieces. Jesus said, "My body is like this bread. My body will be **broken** at My death."

Jesus took a cup of juice made from grapes. He gave the cup to His disciples. All of them drank some of the juice. Jesus said, "My blood is like this juice. My blood will pour out of Me at My death."

The death of Jesus is important. Jesus died to save us from sin. Sin separates us from God. Sin causes us to disobey God. We cannot be friends with God because of sin.

God wants to be our friend. So He sent Jesus to die for our sins. God forgives our sins through the blood of Jesus. Now we can be friends with God.

Today, Christians have a special time of worship. We eat bread. We drink the juice of grapes. We call this time the **Lord's Supper**. We also call it **Communion**. Jesus said, "... do this **in remembrance of** Me."

Christians remember the death of Jesus during **Communion**. We remember that Jesus died for all our sins. We think of His body that was **broken**. We think of His blood that was poured out. We remember how much Jesus loves us. We remember that Jesus will come again. We take **Communion in remembrance** of Him.

The **Lord's Supper** is a good time to pray. We can ask God to show us any sin. He can show us what we should change in our lives. He can help us live better lives. God will help us love Him more.

QUESTIONS: *Fill in the blanks.*

1. The **Passover** helped the_____remember how
   _____helped them leave Egypt.
2. Jesus talked about His_____during the **Passover**.
3. Jesus said, "My body will be_____at My death."
4. Jesus said, "My blood will_____ _____
   at My death."
5. We also call the **Lord's Supper**_____.

Give the answers.

6. What is the name of the special meal the Jews eat each year?
   _____.
7. What separates us from God?_____.
8. Whom did God send to die for our sin?_____.
9. Why is the death of Jesus important? Because Jesus died
   to_____ _____ _____ _____.
10. Why do we have **Communion** today? Give two answers.
    (1) We remember_____.
    (2) We remember_____.

WORD LIST

1. **broken** *(verb):* beaten and hurt and bleeding; killed.
2. **Communion** (kuh-MYEWN-yun) *(proper noun):* the **Lord's Supper**; a special way Christians remember the death of Jesus Christ; a special time of worship for Christians.
3. **in remembrance of** *(prepositional phrase):* to remember; to think of again.
4. **Lord's Supper** *(proper noun phrase):* **Communion**; a special way Christians remember the death of Jesus Christ; a special time of worship for Christians.
5. **Passover** *(proper noun):* a special meal of the Jews once a year. (The Jews remember that God helped them to leave Egypt. The angel of death "passed over" the homes of the Jews. You can read this story in Exodus 12.)

24 JESUS ACCEPTED GOD'S WILL

Memory Verse: ". . . not what I will, but what You [God] will."
   (Mark 14:36)
Scripture: Mark 14:32-42

The Passover meal ended. Jesus and His disciples went outside the city. They went to a garden named Gethsemane (geth-SEM-uh-nee).

Jesus asked His disciples to wait for Him. He said, "Sit here while I pray." He went to another place in Gethsemane. He was tired. He was sad. He wanted to pray to God, His Father.

Jesus knew that He would soon die. He would die on a cross. He would die for the sins of all people. Jesus knew that death on a cross was a terrible death.

Jesus fell to the ground and prayed. He asked God, "Take this cup from Me." "This cup" meant all the suffering Jesus would soon have. Yet He prayed to God, "Do what You want. I want what You want." Jesus chose to accept the will of God.

Jesus returned to His disciples. He wanted them to help Him pray for strength. But they were sleeping. This made Jesus sadder. He felt all alone in His pain and **sorrow**.

Jesus went and prayed again. Then He returned to the disciples. They were sleeping again.

Jesus returned to pray once more. After that, He went to the disciples. He said, "Rise! Let us go!" He was ready for His pain and **sorrow**. He was ready for His death on the Cross. God's will was His will.

Jesus received strength because He prayed to God. Jesus always asked God, His Father, for help. God had always helped Him. He knew God would help Him on the Cross.

Today, Christians must accept God's will. We must do what God wants. We must obey God. But this is not always easy. Sometimes God's will is not what we want. But we must accept God's will because we love Him.

Sometimes Christians have to suffer for their faith. Other people may **persecute** Christians. They may hurt Christians with **unkind** words. They may hurt our bodies. They may even kill us.

Yet, God will help us. We can ask Him for help. He will help us when people **persecute** us. He will help us when people say **unkind** words to us. He will give us strength to do His will. God's will must also be our will.

QUESTIONS: *Fill in the blanks.*

1. Jesus went to a_____named Gethsemane.
2. Jesus went to Gethsemane to_____to God.
3. Jesus asked God, "Take this_____from Me."
4. "This cup" meant all the_____that Jesus would have.
5. Jesus chose to accept_____.
6. Sometimes, Christians have to suffer for their_____.

Answer YES or NO. Circle the right answer.

7. Should Christians accept God's will?   YES or NO
8. Is it always easy to do God's will?   YES or NO
9. Do Christians sometimes have **sorrow**?   YES or NO
10. Will God help us when we ask Him?   YES or NO

WORD LIST

1. **persecute** *(verb):* cause to suffer; cause hurt to people because of what they believe.
2. **sorrow** *(noun):* being very, very sad; a great feeling of being sad.
3. **unkind** *(adjective):* not kind; not nice; bad; evil.

25 JESUS WAS BETRAYED

Memory Verse: "... I live by faith in the Son of God, who loved me and gave **Himself** for me." (Galatians 2:20)
Scripture: Mark 14:43-46, 53, 60-72

Jesus was with His disciples in Gethsemane. One disciple named Judas (JEW-dus) was not with them. Suddenly, Judas came with a crowd. The crowd had **swords** and large sticks of wood. The leaders of the Jews sent the crowd to **arrest** Jesus.

Judas had made a plan with the men. He said, "The man I **kiss** is the person you want. He is Jesus. Then, you can **arrest** Him."

Judas went to Jesus and **kissed** Him. Judas was **himself** a disciple of Jesus. Yet, he was not true to Jesus. He **betrayed** the Son of God.

The men with **swords arrested** Jesus. They took Him to the leaders of the Jews. Other men hit Jesus. They spit on Him. Jesus suffered much.

Peter was another disciple. He was **himself** a good friend of Jesus. But Peter ran away when the men **arrested** Jesus. Peter was afraid.

Later, a girl asked Peter if he knew Jesus. Peter told her that he did not know Jesus. Two more times, people asked Peter if he knew Jesus. Again, Peter said he did not know Jesus.

Peter was like Judas. Peter **betrayed** Jesus. Peter was not willing to say that He knew the Lord. Later, Peter asked God to forgive him. But Judas did not ask God to forgive him.

Today, people can be like Judas and Peter. We can **betray** Jesus. Even Christians sometimes **betray** the Son of God.

How can Christians **betray** Jesus? We **betray** Him when we sin. We **betray** Him when we do not obey Him. We **betray** Him when we are unkind. We **betray** Him when we are not true to Him.

We **betray** Jesus when we do not witness for Him. We may be like Peter. Sometimes we choose to be quiet. We do not speak for Jesus. Sometimes our acts are unkind. Our acts do not show the love of Jesus.

We should not **betray** Jesus. We should be true to Him. Our words and acts should show our love for Jesus.

QUESTIONS: *Fill in the blanks.*

1. Judas had a_____with him to_____Jesus.
2. Judas **betrayed** Jesus with a_____.
3. Peter said_____times that he did not know Jesus.
4. Both Judas and Peter_____
   Jesus.
5. Today, Christians can also **betray**_____.
6. Name two ways we can **betray** Jesus today.
   (1)_____.
   (2)_____.

Answer with YES or NO. Circle the right answer.

7. Was Judas true to Jesus?   YES or NO
8. Was Peter true to Jesus?   YES or NO
9. Can Christians **betray** Jesus?   YES or NO
10. Have you **betrayed** Jesus?   YES or NO

WORD LIST

1. **arrest, arrested** *(verb):* put in jail for not obeying the law. (Police usually arrest people.)
2. **betray, betrayed** *(verb):* not true to; choose not to be a friend any longer. (In this lesson, Judas helped the people who hated Jesus. Judas gave Jesus to people who were not His friends.)
3. **himself, Himself** *(pronoun):* him; the same person as he. (In the memory verse, **Himself** is the Son of God or Jesus Christ.)
4. **kiss** *(verb):* touch another person with the lips. (The Jews often **kissed** another person on the side of the face. It was their way to say "hello.")
5. **swords** *(noun):* long, large knives; tools sometimes used in war or fighting.

26 JESUS CHRIST DIED FOR ALL PEOPLE

Memory Verse: "... Christ died for our sins ..." (1 Corinthians 15:3)
Scripture: Mark 15:21-37
Background Scripture: Mark 15:1-20

The crowd took Jesus to the leaders of the Jews. These leaders were angry with Jesus. They wanted to kill Him. So they took Him to Pilate (PIE-lut). Pilate was the ruler in that country.

Pilate did not want to kill Jesus. Pilate could save the life of Jesus. But the crowd shouted, **"Crucify** Jesus!" Pilate wanted to make the crowd happy. So Pilate let the soldiers take Jesus to **crucify** Him.

The soldiers beat Jesus. They put the robe of a king on Jesus. They put a **crown** of thorns on His head. They made fun of Jesus. They hit Him on the head with a stick. They spat on Him.

The soldiers made Jesus walk to Golgotha (GAHL-guh-thuh). Golgotha was a hill near Jerusalem. Jesus could not carry the heavy Cross. He was hurt and tired. His back was bleeding. The soldiers made another man carry the heavy Cross.

On Golgotha, the soldiers **crucified** Jesus. They nailed Jesus to the Cross. They put the Cross into a hole in the ground. Jesus hung on the Cross. He felt alone and **forsaken**.

Jesus suffered much pain on the Cross. He wore the **crown** of thorns. His hands and feet had nails in them. His blood poured out of His body. Jesus cried out, "... My God, My God, why have You **forsaken** Me?" (verse 34) Then He died.

The plan of God for sin was done. People chose to be sinners. They could not save **themselves**. So God sent His Son, Jesus, to earth to save people. Jesus died to save all people from sin.

Jesus was the **sacrifice** for our sins. He died on the Cross. He came to be the blood **sacrifice** for our sins. Jesus never sinned. He was the perfect **sacrifice**.

Today, we do not need blood **sacrifices**. Jesus was our **sacrifice**. The **sacrifice** of Jesus is enough. We do not need any other **sacrifice**. The Bible says, "... we have been made holy through the **sacrifice** of ... Jesus Christ ..." (Hebrews 10:10)

Now, you can ask Jesus to save you. You can ask Him to forgive your sins. You can trust Him to save you from sin and hell. You can trust Jesus to be your Savior. He died for you.

QUESTIONS: *Fill in the blanks.*

1. _____ was the ruler of the country.
2. Pilate let the soldiers take Jesus to_____Him.
3. The soldiers **crucified** Jesus on a _____.
   The place was Golgotha, a_____near Jerusalem.
4. Jesus_____much pain on the Cross. His _____
   poured out of His body.
5. Jesus was the_____for sin.
6. Today, we do not need a_____**sacrifice**.
   The **sacrifice** of_____is enough.
7. You can trust Jesus to be your_____.

Give the answers.

8. Who were angry with Jesus?_____.
9. What are three things the soldiers did to Jesus?
   (1) _____.
   (2)_____.
   (3)_____.
10. Why did Jesus die on the Cross? To save all people from
   _____.
11. Why was Jesus the perfect **sacrifice**? He never_____.
12. Who is the only One who can save us?_____.

WORD LIST

1. **crown** *(noun):* a type of hat worn by a king or queen. (The soldiers gave Jesus a crown made of sharp thorns. The soldiers put it on Jesus. They made fun of Jesus and called Him a king.)
2. **crucify, crucified** *(verb):* put to death by hanging on a cross.
3. **forsaken** *(verb):* left alone; turn and go away from.
4. **sacrifice, sacrifices** *(noun):* a gift that people give to God. (Jesus was the **sacrifice** or gift to save people from sin.)
5. **themselves** *(pronoun):* them; the same persons as they.

27 JESUS LIVES TODAY

Memory Verse: " . . . He [Jesus] **has risen**! . . ." (Mark 16:6)
Scripture: Mark 15:42—16:8

Jesus Christ was dead. He died on the Cross. Some of His followers were with Him. They saw Jesus die. They knew that He was dead.

A man named Joseph (JOH-zuf) wanted to **bury** Jesus. Joseph asked Pilate for the body of Jesus. Pilate gave the body of Jesus to Joseph. He **buried** Jesus in a tomb. Then, Joseph shut the tomb with a large stone.

Some women saw where Joseph **buried** Jesus. They thought Jesus would stay in the tomb. Many people agreed with the women. Jesus, their Lord, was dead.

After the **Sabbath**, three women went to the tomb. They saw that the tomb was open. Someone had moved the stone. They looked into the tomb. They saw that Jesus was not there. The women were afraid.

The women went into the tomb. They saw a man with white clothes. The man told the women that Jesus was alive. The man said, ". . . He **has risen**! He is not here. . . ." The women saw that Jesus was gone.

Jesus Christ was alive. This was **wonderful** news! The resurrection of Jesus was real. Jesus told His disciples that He would die. He said that He would live again. Jesus did what He promised.

Today, Jesus Christ, the Son of God, lives. This is **wonderful** news! We will never hear better news. We do not worship and serve a dead Jesus. We worship and serve a living Lord.

We **celebrate** the resurrection of Jesus on **Easter**. **Easter** is on the Christian **Sabbath**. On **Easter**, we remember that Jesus **has risen** from death. We **celebrate** because Jesus is alive. Jesus lives today!

QUESTIONS: *Fill in the blanks.*

1. Jesus was _____. He died on the_____.
2. Joseph took the body to_____it.
3. Three women saw that_____was not in the tomb.
4. The man in the tomb told the women that Jesus_____
   _____.
5. The_____of Jesus was real.

Answer with YES or NO. Circle the right answer.

6. Did the people think that Jesus would come
   back to life?   YES or NO
7. Is the resurrection of Jesus **wonderful** news?   YES or NO
8. Do we worship and serve a dead Jesus?   YES or NO
9. Do we **celebrate** the birth of Jesus on **Easter**? YES or NO
10. Is Jesus alive today?   YES or NO

WORD LIST

1. **bury, buried** *(verb):* put a dead body into a tomb or into the ground.
2. **celebrate** *(verb):* remember and honor a special day. (On Easter, Christians **celebrate** the resurrection of Jesus.)
3. **Easter** *(proper noun):* the day each year that Christians **celebrate** the resurrection of Jesus; the special **Sabbath** that Christians remember Jesus came back to life again.
4. **has risen** *(verb phrase):* is alive; has come back to life from death; has left the tomb.
5. **Sabbath** (SAB-uth) *(proper noun):* the day each week the Jews rest and worship God. (The **Sabbath** for the Jews is the last day of the week. The Christian **Sabbath** is the first day of the week.)
6. **wonderful** *(adjective):* great; very, very good.

28 JESUS SAID TO BE HIS WITNESSES

Memory Verse: " . . . Go into all the world and preach the gospel to all **creation**." (Mark 16:15)
Scripture: Mark 16:14-16, 19-20

Jesus was alive. Some people saw Him. But some disciples **doubted**. They did not believe that He was alive.

One day, Jesus **appeared** to the disciples. They saw Him. Now, they could believe too. They could not **doubt** His resurrection.

Jesus **appeared** and talked to His disciples. He said that He was going to leave them. He was going back to heaven. He was going to God, His Father.

Jesus told the disciples what they were to do. He told them to go into all the world. He told them to share the good news with all **creation**. They were to share the good news with all people. Jesus told them to be **witnesses** for Him. (Acts 1:7-8)

Then, Jesus left the disciples. He went up into heaven. Now, Jesus is with God. He is sitting at the right side of God.

God planned that people would share the gospel message. Jesus said to tell the good news to all His **creation**. The disciples obeyed. They preached the gospel where they went. Christians have shared the gospel for many years. Today, Christians still share the gospel.

Jesus saves Christians from all their sins. Christians should share this good news with other people. We are **witnesses** when we share the gospel. We are doing what Jesus told us to do.

Christians can be **witnesses** today. We can witness by our acts and by our words. People hear what we say. People see the things we do. We are **witnesses** with our lives.

Christians are sometimes afraid to share the gospel. But Jesus Christ said, " . . . Do not be afraid. Go and tell . . ." (Matthew 28:10) Jesus has promised to be with us. He has promised to help us.

Christians should be **witnesses** every day. Jesus is coming again. He will **appear** again some day. We must witness to as many people as we can. We must obey our Lord. We must be true to Jesus until He comes again.

QUESTIONS: *Give the answers.*

1. Where did Jesus tell His disciples to go? Into all the
   _____.

2. What did Jesus tell His disciples to do?_____the
   _____ _____with all **creation**.

3. Where is Jesus now? He is_____ _____.

4. What do we do when we share the gospel? We
   _____.

5. How can we be **witnesses?**_____ _____.

Answer with YES or NO. Circle the right answer.

6. Did some disciples **doubt** the resurrection
   of Jesus?   YES or NO

7. Were the disciples **witnesses** for Jesus?   YES or NO

8. Should we keep the good news just for ourselves? YES or NO

9. Do we need to be afraid to witness?   YES or NO

10. Are you a **witness** for Jesus Christ?   YES or NO

WORD LIST

1. **appear, appeared** *(verb):* came so people can see. (Jesus **appeared** or came to the disciples so they could see Him.)

2. **creation** *(noun):* all people that God has made; all the people on the earth.

3. **doubt, doubted** *(verb):* not certain; not know for sure; not know if something is real or has happened.

4. **witness, witnesses** *(noun):* a person who tells what Jesus Christ has done for him or her; people who tell other people the good news of the gospel.

29 HOW TO BECOME A CHRISTIAN

Are you a Christian? Do you know that Jesus **saves** you now? Can you answer "yes"? That is great! But is your answer "no"? Then, you can become a Christian. You can be **saved** now.

Here is what you must do:

1. You must believe that Jesus Christ is the **Savior**. You must believe that He can **save** you.
   "... Believe in the Lord Jesus and you will be **saved** .. ." (Acts 16:31, NCV)

2. You must tell Jesus Christ that you are **sorry** for your sins. "The kind of sorrow God wants makes people change their hearts and lives. This leads to **salvation**." (2 Corinthians 7:10, NCV)

3. You must **repent** of your sins. You must change the way you are living. "So you must change your hearts and lives! Come back to God, and He will **forgive** your sins." (Acts 3:19, NCV)

4. You must ask Jesus Christ to **forgive** your sins. "**Forgive** us for our sins . . ." (Luke 11:4, NCV)

5. You must believe that God **forgives** you through Jesus Christ. "All who believe in Jesus will be **forgiven of their** sins through Jesus. . . ." (Acts 10:43, NCV)

6. You must receive Jesus Christ into your heart and life. "To all who did **accept** Him and believe in Him He gave the **right** to become children of God." (John 1:12, NCV)

Would you pray this prayer?

God, I know I am a **sinner**. I have sinned against You. I am **sorry** for my sins. I **repent** of my sins. Please **forgive** me for all my sins. I now believe that You **forgive** me. Come into my life. Help me not to sin again. I believe that Jesus Christ is my **Savior**. Thank You for **saving** me from sin. I now **accept** Jesus as my **Savior**. I now receive Jesus Christ into my heart and life. Thank You, God. I have the **right** to be Your child. **Amen.**

Now, tell another person today that Jesus Christ **saves** you. The Bible says, "All those who stand before others and say they believe in Me [Jesus], I, the Son of Man, will say before the angels of God that they belong to Me." (Luke 12:8, NCV) You should tell other people about your **salvation**. You should tell what Jesus has done for you. This will help you to grow as a Christian.

WORD LIST

1. **accept** *(verb):* agree to receive; agree in your mind and heart.
2. **amen** *(interjection):* a word used at the end of prayers. (**Amen** means *yes, it is true.* **Amen** shows that we agree with what was said.)
3. **forgive, forgives, forgiven** *(verb):* make free from the shame for sins; choose to forget the wrong things that people do.
4. **repent** *(verb):* stop doing sins; turn from a life of sin and turn to God.
5. **right** *(noun):* something that we can say is ours. (We have the **right** not to be hurt by another person. As Christians, we have the **right** to be children of God.)
6. **salvation** *(noun):* the act of God by which He **saves** people from sin.
7. **save, saves, saving** *(verb),* **saved** *(adjective):* make free from sin; not punish a person for his or her sin.
8. **Savior** (SAYV-yer) *(proper noun):* Jesus Christ, the Son of God; the One who came to **save** people from their sins and hell.
9. **sorry** *(adjective):* be very sad about your sins.

INTRODUCTION FOR TEACHERS

The *intercultural English* lessons in this book are written for people who are developing proficiency in English. The intended audience includes bilingual speakers, such as new immigrants and ESL (English as a second language) learners, and English speakers who are preliterate or learning disabled. Also, new Christians and people with a limited knowledge of Bible truths can benefit by the simple, brief lessons. Such people can profit from materials with a controlled vocabulary and sentence structure to help them better understand the Bible and Christian concepts.

The target audience is the beginning-level student who can work comfortably with an 800-word vocabulary. The writers, therefore, gave careful consideration to both the vocabulary and sentence structure.

New words and phrases, 10 or less, are introduced in each lesson. The words/phrases are in the word lists in the same form or forms as in the lesson text. The parts of speech are included as an aid for teaching English.

In applying linguistic controls, the language is simplified. The writers purposely sacrificed style for simplicity to obtain English at a level that is more easily read by the target audience.

The lessons, based on previously written Bible studies, are adapted to *intercultural English* to serve as transition materials while the learners are gaining Bible knowledge and English skills. The adaptation also involved deleting language and content (such as illustrations, examples, poetry, and so on) that may be inappropriate in a cross-cultural learning situation.

There are three appendixes in this section, *Teacher Resources*. Appendix A contains suggested answers to the study questions. Appendix B includes all the vocabulary introduced in the lessons. Appendix C includes several useful tips for teaching. Teachers should become familiar with this supplementary information.

Teachers need to be sensitive to the work of the Holy Spirit. Lesson 29, "How to Become a Christian," may be used at any time a student is ready to accept Jesus Christ as Savior.

We believe simple Bible study material meets a vital need in Christian churches today. We pray that God will honor His Word as it becomes a part of the learners' minds and hearts.

J. Wesley Eby, *editor*

APPENDIX A
ANSWERS TO QUESTIONS

For each lesson there is a set of suggested answers for the study questions. You will find the intended answers, along with some possible alternatives or extensions (in parentheses), which are all correct in the context of the lessons. Accept any answer that can be justified.

Lesson 1
1. Jesus (Christ)
2. good news; sins
3. Mark (also Matthew, Luke, or John)
4. Jesus (Christ)
5. Bethlehem
6. Scripture
7. Yes
8. No
9. Yes
10. Yes

Lesson 2
1. Father; loves
2. Mary; God
3. Son; God (Man)
4. repent
5. come
6. John (the Baptist)
7. Holy Spirit
8. My Son
9. God; Christians (believers)
10. Jesus (Christ); Son of Man

Lesson 3
1. desert
2. Satan
3. sin
4. temptation(s) (Satan)
5. no
6. Yes
7. No
8. Yes
9. No
10. Yes

Lesson 4
1. (in) Galilee
2. Follow Me
3. Peter; Andrew
4. James; John
5. Zebedee
6. follow
7. obey
8. (Holy) Bible
9. God
10. sermons (pastors; preachers)

Lesson 5
1. Capernaum
2. many people (more and more people)
3. hole (roof; hole in the roof)
4. faith
5. forgive; sins
6. healed
7. Yes
8. No
9. Yes
10. Yes
11. [personal response]

Lesson 6
1. Pharisees
2. holy
3. Jesus
4. sinners
5. God
6. sinners (God)
7. Yes
8. Yes
9. No
10. No

Lesson 7
1. helped (loved; healed; etc.)
2. crowd
3. love
4. Jesus; hope
5. people
6. love; obey
7. (1) healed;
   (2) encouraged
8. mother; brothers (family)
9. will

Lesson 8
1. stories; parables
2. seeds
3. (1) hard
   (2) stones
   (3) weeds
   (4) good
4. Word; God
5. hear (obey)
6. Yes
7. No
8. Yes
9. Yes

Lesson 9
1. Lake Galilee
2. storm
3. sleeping
4. stopped
5. peace
6. Jesus (God)
7. Yes
8. Yes
9. No
10. [personal response]

Lesson 10
1. evil spirit (demon)
2. problems
3. out
4. power
5. well (healed)
6. overcome
7. Many
8. God (Jesus)
9. God (Jesus)
10. tell other people (witness for God)

Lesson 11
1. daughter
2. faith
3. power; alive
4. hell
5. heaven
6. Jesus (Christ)
7. No
8. No
9. Yes
10. No

Lesson 12
1. powerful
2. afraid
3. trust
4. things (wind; water)
5. courage
6. afraid
7. Yes
8. Yes
9. No
10. [personal response]

Lesson 13
1. Ten Commandments
2. disobeyed (not obeyed)
3. obey
4. sin (evil; evil thoughts)
5. Jesus (Christ; God)
6. No
7. No
8. Yes
9. Yes
10. [personal response]

Lesson 14
1. food
2. sad; eat (have food)
3. thanked
4. kind; loves
5. miracles
6. 4,000
7. 7 (seven)
8. (all the) people (everyone)
9. Jesus (God)
10. Jesus (God)

Lesson 15
1. follow
2. yes
3. forever
4. separates
5. Savior
6. No
7. Yes
8. Yes
9. No
10. No

Lesson 16
1. predicted
2. argued (were arguing)
3. selfish
4. first
5. last; other people
6. servant; serve
7. death; resurrection
8. die; sins
9. Jesus
10. witness for Jesus (tell other people what Jesus has done for us) [Other answers are possible.]

Lesson 17

1. rich
2. eternal life
3. laws
4. sell
5. difficult
6. willing
7. Jesus (God)
8. all things (eternal life)
9. eternal life
10. Yes
11. No
12. [personal response]

Lesson 18

1. three (3)
2. Jerusalem
3. colt
4. praise
5. King; lives
6. Psalms
7. Praise the Lord
8. Yes
9. No
10. No
11. No
12. [personal response]

Lesson 19

1. law
2. love God
3. neighbors
4. witness
5. kind acts
6. heart; soul; mind; strength
7. God
8. God
9. our neighbors (other people)

Lesson 20

1. troubles (problems; wars; famines; earthquakes)
2. hate; follow
3. easy
4. true
5. friend; suffering (troubles)
6. saved
7. Yes
8. Yes
9. No
10. [personal response]

Lesson 21

1. come back (come again)
2. terrible
3. saved people (Christians)
4. God (the Father)
5. ready; late
6. Christian; Jesus; Savior
7. No
8. No
9. Yes
10. [personal response]

Lesson 22

1. Simon
2. perfume
3. beautiful
4. tomb
5. love
6. Jesus

7. families; friends (people; things we own)
8. Bethany (in the town of Bethany)
9. perfume; food
10. [Any of these answers are correct. There are other possible answers.] We can give Him our praise and worship. We can give Jesus our service. We can give Him our love. We can give Jesus our lives.

Lesson 23
1. Jews; God
2. death
3. broken
4. pour out
5. Communion
6. Passover
7. sin
8. Jesus (Christ)
9. save us from sin
10. [Any of these answers are correct.] the death of Jesus; that Jesus died for all our sins; how much Jesus loves us; that Jesus will come again

Lesson 24
1. garden
2. pray
3. cup
4. suffering
5. God's will (the will of God)

6. faith
7. Yes
8. No
9. Yes
10. Yes

Lesson 25
1. crowd; arrest
2. kiss
3. three (3)
4. betrayed
5. Jesus (Christ)
6. [Any of these answers are correct. There are other possible answers.] when we sin; when we do not obey Him [Jesus]; when we are not true to Him [Jesus]; when we do not witness for Him [Jesus]; when our acts do not show the love of Jesus
7. No
8. No
9. Yes
10. [personal response]

Lesson 26
1. Pilate
2. crucify (kill)
3. cross; hill
4. suffered; blood
5. (perfect) sacrifice
6. blood; Jesus (Christ)
7. Savior
8. (the) leaders of the Jews
9. [Any of these answers are correct.] They

whipped Him. They put the robe of a king on Him. They put a crown of thorns on His head. They made fun of Him. They hit Him on the head with a stick. They spat on Him. They killed (crucified) Him.

10. sin
11. sinned
12. Jesus (Christ)

Lesson 27

1. dead; Cross
2. bury
3. Jesus
4. was alive
5. resurrection
6. No
7. Yes
8. No
9. No
10. Yes

Lesson 28

1. world
2. share; good news
3. with God (in heaven; sitting at the right side of God)
4. witness [Other answers are possible.]
5. with our lives (by our acts; by our words)
6. Yes
7. Yes
8. No
9. No
10. [personal response]

Lesson 29

[There are no questions and answers.]

APPENDIX B
WORD LIST

Below is an alphabetical list of all the words and phrases in the Word Lists in this book. The number after each entry indicates the lesson where the word or phrase was introduced.

accept, accepted *(verb):* agree to receive; agree in your mind and heart. [13 and 29]

alabaster (AL-uh-BAS-ter) *(adjective):* a type of stone used to make pretty jars and other things. [22]

amaze, amazed *(verb):* to surprise in a great way; did something that is hard to understand. [12]

amen *(interjection):* a word used at the end of prayers. (**Amen** means, *Yes, it is true.* **Amen** shows that we agree with what was said.) [29]

appear, appeared *(verb):* came so people can see. (Jesus **appeared** or came to the disciples so they could see Him.) [28]

argued, arguing *(verb):* fighting with words; not agreeing with. [16]

arrest, arrested *(verb):* put in jail for not obeying the law, (Police usually arrest people.) [25]

background Scripture *(noun phrase):* some Scripture from the Bible; other Scripture to help us better understand the lesson. [2]

baptize, baptized *(verb):* put under water and lifted out of water. [2]

beautiful *(adjective):* very good; very kind; very nice. [22]

betray, betrayed *(verb):* not true to; choose not to be a friend any longer. (In this lesson, Judas helped the people who hated Jesus. Judas gave Jesus to people who were not His friends.) [25]

broken *(verb):* beaten and hurt and bleeding; killed. [23]

bury, buried *(verb):* put a dead body into a tomb or into the ground. [27]

calm *(adjective):* not moving; quiet; no wind blowing; having peace inside us. [9]

celebrate *(verb):* remember and honor a special day. (On Easter, Christians **celebrate** the resurrection of Jesus.) [27]

colt *(noun):* a young horse. [18]

come back *(verb phrase):* return; come again. (In this lesson, **come back** means that Jesus will return to earth.) [21]

command, commands, commanded *(verb):* tell someone to do something; told someone to obey. [13]

Communion (kuh-MYEWN-yun) *(proper noun):* the Lord's Supper; a special way Christians remember the death of Jesus Christ; a special time of worship for Christians. [23]

courage *(noun):* not be afraid; being strong inside of you when you are afraid; being strong inside when you have troubles. [12]

creation *(noun):* all people that God has made; all the people on the earth. [28]

cross *(noun)*, **Cross** *(proper noun):* a tool, made of two pieces of wood, used for killing people; usually has the shape of the letter T. (Jesus died by hanging on a **cross**.) [15]

crown *(noun):* a type of hat worn by a king or queen. (The soldiers gave Jesus a **crown** made of sharp thorns. The soldiers put it on Jesus. They made fun of Jesus and called Him a king.) [26]

crucify, crucified *(verb):* put to death by hanging on a cross. [26]

daughter *(noun):* a girl child of a mother and father. [11]

demon, demons *(noun):* an evil spirit; a bad spirit that works against God and for Satan. [10]

difficult *(adjective):* not easy; hard to do. [17]

disciples *(noun):* people who follow and obey Jesus Christ. (The 12 men Jesus chose to be His special **disciples**.) [6]

disliked *(verb):* did not like; did not love. [6]

disobey, disobeyed *(verb):* did not obey; did not do what God told them to do. [13]

don't *(contraction):* do not. [9]

doubt *(verb):* not certain; not know for sure; not know if something is real or has happened. [28]

dove *(noun):* a type of small bird that is white or gray. [2]

drown *(verb):* die by being under water too long. [9]

earn *(verb):* work for; do something to get something else. [17]

earthquakes *(noun):* the earth or ground shaking and moving. [20]

Easter *(proper noun):* the day each year that Christians celebrate the resurrection of Jesus; the special Sabbath that Christians remember Jesus came back to life again. [27]

encouraged *(verb):* made people feel better; helped people in their spirits. [7]

eternal life *(noun phrase).* the life that God gives; the life with God now and life with God forever in heaven [11]

evil spirit, evil spirits *(noun phrase):* a demon; bad spirits that work against God and for Satan. [10]

expect *(verb):* think something will happen. [20]

extra *(adjective):* more than is needed; more than enough. [14]

faith *(noun):* belief in God; believing that God can do great things. [5]

famines *(noun):* times when there is little or no food; times when people are sick or die because they are hungry. [20]

first *(adjective):* very important; the most important person. [16]

fishermen *(noun):* people who catch fish for a job. [4]

followers *(noun):* Christians; people who believe in Jesus Christ and follow Him; people who obey what Jesus taught. [20]

forever *(adverb):* time that has no end; time that goes on and on and on. [11]

forgive, forgives *(verb):* make free from the shame for sins; choose to forget the wrong things that people do. [1 and 29]

forgiven *(verb):* made free from the shame for sin; God choosing to forget our sins. [5 and 29]

forsaken *(verb):* left alone; turn and go away from. [26]

for sure *(prepositional phrase):* for certain; something that will happen. [21]

Galilee *(proper noun):* a part of the country where Jesus lived; also, the name of a large lake in this country. [4]

ghost *(noun):* the spirit of a dead person. [12]

glory *(noun):* a word that tells us about God. (**Glory** means how great and important God is.) [21]

God's will *(noun phrase):* what God wants for all people. [7]

good news *(noun phrase):* the story that Jesus Christ can save people from their sins. [1]

Gospel, Gospels *(proper noun):* the first four books of the New Testament in the Bible. (The **Gospels** tell the good news about Jesus Christ. **Gospel** means "good news.") [1]

has risen *(verb phrase):* is alive; has come back to life from death; has left the tomb. [27]

heal, healed *(verb):* make well; helped people not be sick any longer. [5]

heaven *(noun):* the home of God. (**Heaven** is also where Christians live after death.) [2]

hell *(noun):* the home of sinners after they die; a place where God punishes people forever for their sins. [11]

himself, Himself *(pronoun):* him; the same person as he. (In the memory verse, **Himself** is the Son of God or Jesus Christ.) [25]

Holy Bible *(proper noun):* the 66 books that God gave us to learn about Him; the written Word of God; the Scripture. [1]

Holy Spirit *(proper noun):* the spirit of God. [2]

hope *(noun):* believing that God will do what He says He will do; believing in life after death. [7]

hosanna (hoh-ZAH-nuh) *(noun):* "save" or "save us"; a word used to show praise to Jesus Christ. [18]

impossible *(adjective):* not possible; cannot happen; not able to be done. [17]

in remembrance of *(prepositional phrase):* to remember; to think of again. [23]

Jews *(proper noun):* the people of the country of Israel. [6]

keep, kept *(verb):* obey; do what the laws and rules say to do. [6]

kiss *(verb):* touch another person with the lips. (The Jews often **kissed** another person on the side of the face. It was their way to say "hello.") [25]

last *(adjective):* not very important; the least important person. [16]

leaders *(noun):* people who lead or rule other people. (**Leaders** are sometimes rulers of nations or groups of people.) [20]

loaves *(noun):* more than one loaf of bread. (A loaf is a large piece of bread before it is cut into smaller pieces.) [14]

Lord's Supper *(proper noun phrase):* Communion; a special way Christians remember the death of Jesus Christ; a special time of worship for Christians. [23]

meet all your needs, meet all our needs *(verb phrase):* give you everything that you need; do for you something that needs to be done. [14]

message *(noun):* a written or spoken way to share some news. [2]

mighty *(adjective):* great; very strong; with much power. [10]

miracle, miracles *(noun):* something that happens only with the help of God; something that people cannot do without the help of God. [2]

myself *(pronoun):* me; the same person as I. [19]

neighbors *(noun):* people living near you. (In this lesson, **neighbors** can also mean any people.) [19]

ourselves *(pronoun):* us; the same persons as you and me. [1]

overcome *(verb):* be stronger than; have more power than. [10]

palm *(noun):* a type of tree. (**Palm** trees grow where the weather is warm all year.) [18]

Palm Sunday *(proper noun phrase):* the Sunday before Easter; the special day Christians remember Jesus riding a colt into Jerusalem. [18]

parable, parables *(noun):* a short story that teaches a lesson. (**Parables** help people understand things about God and the Christian life.) [8]

paralyzed *(adjective):* cannot move a part of the body; cannot walk or use the hands. [5]

Passover *(proper noun):* a special meal of the Jews once a year. (The Jews remember that God helped them to leave Egypt. The angel of death "passed over" the homes of the Jews. You can read this story in Exodus 12.) [23]

pastors *(noun):* people who preach about God. (**Pastors** often preach in churches. **Pastors** are also preachers.) [4]

perfume *(noun):* something that has a nice smell. (People put **perfume** on their bodies to make them smell nice.) [22]

persecute *(verb):* cause to suffer; cause hurt to people because of what they believe. [24]

Pharisees *(proper noun):* important people in the religion of the Jews; teachers of the law of the Jews. [6]

possible *(adjective):* may happen; may be done. [17]

powerful *(adjective):* with much power; able to do great things. [12]

praised *(verb):* gave thanks to; worshiped; told God how great He is, [5]

preacher *(noun):* a person who tells people about God; a person who tells the good news of Jesus. (A **preacher** often speaks or preaches in a church.) [2]

predict, predicted *(verb):* tell what is going to happen before it happens. [16]

quickly *(adverb):* fast; right away. [4]

rather than *(prepositional phrase):* instead of; in place of. [13]

repent, repented *(verb):* stop doing sins; turn from a life of sin and turn to God. [2 and 29]

resurrection *(noun):* living again after death; coming back to life after dying. [16]

right *(noun):* something that we can say is ours. (We have the **right** not to be hurt by another person. As Christians, we have the **right** to be children of God.) [29]

rule *(verb):* control; be in charge of our lives. [18]

ruler *(noun):* a person who leads other people; a person who writes rules or laws. [11]

Sabbath (SAB-uth) *(proper noun):* the day each week the Jews rest and worship God. (The **Sabbath** for the Jews is the last day of the week. The Christian **Sabbath** is the first day of the week.) [27]

sacrifice, sacrifices *(noun):* a gift that people give to God. (Jesus was the **sacrifice** or gift to save people from sin.) [26]

salvation *(noun):* the act of God by which He saves people from sin. [29]

Satan *(proper noun):* the very bad spirit who fights against God; the bad spirit with the most power. [3]

save *(verb):* make free from sin; not punish people for their sins [1]

saved *(adjective):* have eternal life; will not be punished in hell for sin. [17 and 29]

Savior (SAYV-yer) *(proper noun):* Jesus Christ; the Son of God; the One who came to save people from their sins and hell. [13 and 29]

Scripture *(proper noun):* the Holy Bible; the written Word of God; any part of the Bible. [1]

selfish *(adjective):* thinking only of your own self; not thinking about other people. [16]

separates *(verb):* not together; keeps away from. [15]

sermons *(noun):* messages; what preachers or pastors say when they tell us about God. (Pastors often preach **sermons** in church services.) [4]

servant, servants *(noun):* a person who works for or serves other people. [16]

service *(noun):* what people do to serve Jesus; all the things people do to help Jesus on earth. [22]

sickness *(noun):* being sick and feeling bad; not well in our bodies. [9]

sin, sins *(noun):* the acts and thoughts of people against God and His laws; the things people do when they do not obey God. [1]

sinners *(noun):* people who sin; people who do not obey the laws of God. [6]

Son of Man *(proper noun phrase):* Jesus Christ, who was born of a human mother. [2]

sorrow *(noun):* being very, very sad; a great feeling of being sad. [24]

sorry *(adjective):* be very sad about your sins. [29]

soul *(noun):* the part of the person that lives after death. [19]

stand firm, stands firm *(verb phrase):* does not stop believing in God; is true to God. [20]

strength *(noun):* being strong in your spirit; having power inside of you. [19]

suddenly *(adverb):* very fast; quickly. [9]

suffer, suffered *(verb):* have pain; hurt; do without things you think you need. [15]

suffering *(noun):* having pain, trouble, and hurt in life. [20]

swords *(noun):* long, large knives; tools sometimes used in war or in fighting. [25]

synagogue *(noun):* a place of worship for the Jews; a church. [11]

take courage *(verb phrase):* do not be afraid; have courage. [12]

take up your cross, take up our cross *(verb phrase):* follow Jesus; obey God; do everything God wants you to do. [15]

tempt, tempts, tempted *(verb):* try to get a person to sin or do wrong. [3]

temptation, temptations *(noun):* the act of Satan to tempt people; Satan trying to get a person to sin. [3]

Ten Commandments *(proper noun phrase):* important laws that God gave to the Jews through Moses. [13]

terrible *(adjective):* very, very bad; causing great fear. [21]

the righteous *(noun phrase):* good people; people who obey God and His laws; people who do what is right. [6]

themselves *(pronoun):* them; the same persons as they. [26]

tomb *(noun):* a place where we put a dead person. [22]

true *(adjective):* loyal. (In this lesson, **true** means to follow Jesus always. To be **true** means to love and obey Jesus.) [20]

trouble *(noun):* problems; temptations; times of hurt and pain. [8]

turn away from God *(verb phrase):* do not obey God; do not worship God any longer; sin against God. [3]

unkind *(adjective):* not kind; not nice; bad; evil. [24]

whoever *(pronoun):* any person; a man, a woman, a young person, or a child. [7]

witness, witnessed *(verb):* tell people what God has done for you; tell people about Jesus Christ. [10]

witness, witnesses *(noun):* a person who tells what Jesus Christ has done for him or her; people who tell other people the good news of the gospel. [28]

wonderful *(adjective):* great; very, very good. [27]

Word of God *(proper noun phrase):* the Holy Bible; the truth of God; the law of God. [8]

work of God *(noun phrase):* anything that God tells people to do; what God does to help people know and love Him. [1]

worry *(verb):* have no peace in your mind; think about something so much you do not have peace; be afraid of what may happen. [8]

worship *(verb):* obey and serve; give thanks to; give honor to. [3]

yourself *(pronoun):* you; the same person as you. [19]

APPENDIX C
TEACHING HELPS

A. **Plan carefully and prayerfully.** Anything important enough to do is important enough to plan to do. Unplanned teaching usually results in disorganized instruction, resulting in minimal learning. A familiar maxim says, "If I fail to plan, I plan to fail." Your students are worthy of your careful planning and sincere prayers. Commit your teaching and the learners to God. He will help you as you do your best.

B. **Be sensitive to the learners' needs.** Your students will probably be at different levels, both in their Bible knowledge and language skills. Your task, which is not an easy one, is to discover where the learners are in their English skills and in their understanding of the Christian faith.

Be aware, also, that the learners' *felt needs* may be different from their *real needs*. But their *felt needs* usually must be met first before you are able to help them with their *real needs*. In your class, you may find the *felt need* is to learn to read while the *real need* is to learn about God. And while you strive to meet the perceived or *felt need*, never lose sight of the *real need*.

There is no special method to help you make this discovery. You DO need to become a people-watcher, however. Look for any hints the students may give in their body language and in what they say. Also, become involved in the learners' lives, both in and out of class. This will help you become much more aware of their backgrounds, their culture, their experiences, and, thus, their needs, *felt and real*. God will be faithful as you commit this *discovery process* to Him.

C. **Determine your objective.** An objective is the purpose for teaching. Your objective or aim, as a Christian teacher, is twofold: Bible content and English language skills. Knowing *what* you are teaching, and *why*, will help you be more confident as a teacher or tutor. As a result, your instruction will be more effective. Therefore, become familiar with the lesson content and, if possible, the language skills needed by the learners.

D. **Focus on comprehension.** This is extremely important! If the learners do not understand, your instruction will be of limited value. Of course, not every student will fully understand everything you teach. But, as a teacher or tutor, try to have each student take away some learning from each session. How much the students understand and learn will vary from person to person. Yet, your task is to faithfully plant the seeds of God's Word. Then the Holy Spirit will help those seeds to grow and bear fruit in the minds and hearts of the learners.

Some strategies for aiding comprehension are:

1. *Use easy-to-read Bibles.* Some recommended ones are:

   - *The Holy Bible, New Century Version.* Thomas Nelson, Inc., P.O. Box 141000, Nashville, TN 37214

   - *Contemporary English Version.* American Bible Society, 101 N. Independence Mall East FL8, Philadelphia, PA 19106-2155

   - *Good News Translation Bible.* American Bible Society, 101 N. Independence Mall East FL8, Philadelphia, PA 19106-2155

   - *Holy Bible: New Life Version.* Barbour Publishing, 1810 Barbour Dr. SE, Uhrichsville, OH 44683

If the students are not native speakers of English, have them read the Scripture in their first language. This will certainly aid their understanding. Some sources of Bibles in various languages are:

   - AMERICAN BIBLE SOCIETY, 101 N. Independence Mall East FL8, Philadelphia, PA 19106-2155

   - MULTI-LANGUAGE MEDIA, 701 Pennsylvania Ave., Fort Washington, PA 19034

- INTERNATIONAL BIBLE SOCIETY, 1820 Jet Stream Drive, Colorado Springs, CO 80921

- BIBLE LEAGUE INTERNATIONAL, 1 Bible League Plaza, Crete, IL 60417

2. *Use the students' first language also, if their native language is other than English.* This is ideal and will result in the greatest amount of learning. If an interpreter is available, or if you know the language, use both languages in your teaching. If possible, give the interpreter the material to be taught before the class session so he or she can become familiar with the lesson content.

3. *Take additional time to teach a lesson, as needed.* You can divide a lesson into two or more parts, according to the needs of the learners. Remember: You're teaching people, not materials. Materials are only tools by which you accomplish your objectives or aims.

4. *Tell the learners what you plan to teach as you begin a lesson.* Make the students aware of the lesson content at the beginning of the class. Then after you have taught, give a brief review. Thus, the lesson plan should include these three steps: (1) telling what you are going to teach, (2) teaching, and (3) telling what you have just taught.

5. *Involve the students as much as possible.* Most people learn best by doing. Therefore, involve the students in a wide variety of activities: listening, talking, moving, drawing, devising, singing, discussing, cooperating, writing, conversing, exploring, memorizing, manipulating, creating, reciting, etc. Take advantage of all the possible ways students learn.

6. *Use the questions in the lessons as a part of your teaching.* Questions are an important part of teaching. If time permits, use the questions as a part of the lessons. Or if time is limited, assign the questions for home study and discuss them during

the next class session as review and reinforcement. Avoid grading the answers in such a way that the students have a sense of failure. (See Section E.) Note: If the questions are an out-of-class assignment, be aware that other family members or friends may help answer the questions.

7. *Don't assume the learners can read the lessons on their own.* If the learners cannot read English, teach the lessons orally. Once the students seem to be reading independently, don't assume they understand what they are reading. Pronouncing the words does not necessarily mean they can read with comprehension. Use oral questions and discussion to help you determine how much they understand.

8. *Work with new and unknown words both before and during the lesson.* Develop vocabulary in meaningful activities, avoiding word lists. Many of the high-frequency words of English (such as *the, but, or, of, by, because*) have limited or no meaning by themselves. Also, many nouns and verbs have multiple meanings. Vocabulary has little value if there are no useful meanings for the learners. Always work with words in phrases or sentences that have meaning for the students. Make flash cards by writing the new word on the front, and write sentences with the word on the back. Also, be careful in the use of idioms, figures of speech, and slang expressions.

9. *Add your own examples and stories that are appropriate for the lessons.* Nonbiblical examples and stories are not included since such examples and stories are different from culture to culture. Yet, such stories or examples are very effective in the learning process. Just make certain the stories, examples, or illustrations are appropriate and meaningful for your learners.

10. *Use real objects, pictures, and other audiovisual aids, as much as possible.* Bulletin boards, charts, flash cards, models, photographs, videos, etc., will make the lessons more effective.

E. **Teach for success.** This begins, of course, with focusing on comprehension. If the learners understand, then you should expect success.

   1. *Give sincere praise.* Help the students know they are learning. Reinforce their self-worth as individuals and as God's children, created in His image.

   2. *Capitalize on the learners' strengths and their correct responses.* Minimize their weaknesses and mistakes.

   3. *Assume every student WANTS to learn, CAN learn, and WILL learn.* Then teach according to this belief.

F. **Be a good language model.** This is essential since people are introduced to language by listening to it. This is true for all native and most nonnative English speakers. As a language model, however, you do not have to be perfect. Discard any worries you may have. Just be yourself and be the best you can be. Try these practical ideas:

   1. *Be natural.* Use spoken English as it is naturally used by native English speakers. Be careful not to talk down to the learners by using "baby talk."

   2. *Talk slowly.* Most learners, especially second language learners, better understand language if spoken a little slower than used in normal speech. Yet, the speaker must maintain appropriate volume, rhythm, stress, and phrasing. Some teachers err by increasing volume as they slow down their speech. The increased volume is often misinterpreted by the learners.

   3. *Be clear in pronunciation.* Pronounce words distinctly, making certain that you do not omit or slur final consonant sounds. Try to be clear and precise in your pronunciation while retaining naturalness.

Don't expect adults or older youth who are learning English as a second language to speak it as native speakers. Research indicates that the learners will probably always speak it with an accent. Remember: The goal is for the learners to be able to communicate in English. They can accomplish this goal even if their pronunciation is not perfect.

4. *Model correct language.* This is an important technique, especially for correcting mistakes. You can show the correct response, language usage, or pronunciation simply by "doing it" yourself. Don't require the students to correct all their mistakes. For each lesson, focus on only one or two mistakes you would like the learners to correct and master. Pointing out too many errors at a time can be discouraging and embarrassing for the learner.

5. *Read aloud often.* You, as the teacher or tutor, can model good reading and oral language as you read aloud to the students. Research indicates that this is a valuable technique. And as you read, be expressive and enthusiastic.

   Students need to hear you read the Scriptures frequently as well as the entire lesson. Read a Bible passage or the lesson aloud first before the learners ever see it. Then, read it a second time while they follow along with their eyes. This provides them with needed auditory (ear) and visual (eye) introduction to the lesson before they read it on their own

Editor's Note:

This information on teaching is extremely limited. Entire textbooks have been written on this subject. Space requirements, however, require that this supplementary material be brief. I pray, though, that what you have read will assist you as you minister to your students.

J. Wesley Eby

NOTES

NOTES

NOTES

NOTES

NOTES

NOTES

NOTES

NOTES

NOTES

NOTES